LECTIO DIVINA
WITH THE SPIRITUAL MASTERS

The Gospel of John with St. Augustine

LECTIO DIVINA
WITH THE SPIRITUAL MASTERS

The Gospel of John with St. Augustine

Compiled and adapted by
Rev. Peter A. Heasley, SThD

TAN Books
Gastonia, North Carolina

Unless otherwise noted, Scripture quotations are from the Douay-Rheims Bible, available in the Public Domain.

The Gospel of John with St. Augustine exclusively uses, with permission, this translation of St. Augustine's homilies: *Homilies on the Gospel of John 1–40* and *Homilies on the Gospel of John 41–124*, ed. Allan D. Fitzgerald and Boniface Ramsey, trans. Edmund Hill, vol. 12, *The Works of Saint Augustine: A Translation for the 21st Century*, New York City Press.

Compiled and adapted by Rev. Peter A. Heasley, SThD

Cover and interior design by Jordan Avery

Artwork by Chris Lewis, Baritus Catholic Illustration | bartiuscatholic.com

ISBN: 978-1-5051-3551-0
Kindle ISBN: 978-1-5051-3635-7
ePUB ISBN: 978-1-5051-3634-0

Published in the United States by
TAN Books
PO Box 269
Gastonia, NC 28053

www.TANBooks.com

Printed in the United States of America

"Make knowledge of the Scriptures your love . . . Live with them, meditate on them, make them the sole object of your knowledge and inquiries."

—St. Jerome

CONTENTS

PUBLISHER'S INTRODUCTION

What is Lectio Divina?

Lectio Divina, which translates from Latin as "divine reading," is a traditional spiritual practice in Catholicism involving the contemplative reading of scripture. It dates back to the early Christian monastics and was formalized in the 12th century by a Carthusian monk named Guigo II. The process is designed to promote communion with God and to increase the knowledge of God's Word.

> "Lectio divina is a great river that carries all the riches accumulated over the course of Church history by the fervent readers of God's Word. 'Lectio divina' is never solely our own reading. It feeds on the interpretation of those who have preceded us . . .if we persevere in 'lectio divina' and silent listening to what the Spirit is saying to the Churches, our effort will be rewarded by unheard-of jewels and riches."
>
> —Cardinal Robert Sarah

Who is a Spiritual Master?

The Spiritual Masters are those saints who have given the Church spiritual guidance applicable to all generations. The sanctity we are striving for is found in their writings and in their witness as faithful, holy Catholics. We sit at their feet, desiring to know more of this inner life of the Trintiy that began at our Baptism. We want to grow in holiness and become saints.

What is Lectio Divina with the Spiritual Masters?

In the book of Acts, there is the story of the eunuch who encounters Philip. Philip asks the question, "Do you know what you are reading?" The eunuch responds, "How can I unless someone explains it to me?" Many times, Catholics have a similar experience when reading Sacred Scripture alone or trying to do Lectio Divina. Even faithful Catholics go through dry periods of prayer, where it can even be difficult to bring themselves to intentional prayer time.

Fruitful times of prayer and fruitful Lectio Divina usually depend upon knowledge of Scripture and the strength of imaginative prayer. If these two things are lacking in prayer, we may draw very little consolation or direction from the Holy Spirit.

TAN Books has created a structured approach to the books of the Bible with enriching commentary from the spiritual masters, meditations to draw the reader into the story, and relevant prompts based on the text and the wisdom of the saint to draw the reader up and lead them to contemplation. We want Catholics to pray the Scriptures and practice Lectio Divina with the saints whose spiritual guidance is necessary for our sanctity and growth in holiness.

HOW TO USE THIS BOOK

The Steps of Lectio Divina with the Spiritual Masters

1. LECTIO—Read with the Spiritual Masters

The first step is **reading**. Read the passage of Scripture carefully, more than once if needed. You will notice **words in bold** throughout the text. This is to catch your attention because the Spiritual Master will comment on these particular passages. Next, read the **Reading with** ___________ section, which is the commentary on that section of Scripture by the Spiritual Master. The Spiritual Master will guide your prayer of Scripture with insights that will spiritually benefit you in your call to holiness.

2. MEDITATIO—Meditate with the Spiritual Masters

The second step is **meditation**. Building on the Scripture passage and commentary, use your imagination to enter into the Biblical scene in order to prayerfully consider the setting, the people, and the divine action. The *meditatio* section will give your mind material for meditation on both the story of salvation and the Truths of the Catholic Faith. It is through this meditation that you enter the text and discover its further meaning for you.

3.ORATIO—Pray with the Spiritual Masters

The next step is **prayer**. This is your response to the text and meditation. Through prayerful engagement with your needs and intentions, the needs and intentions of others, and the text, offer your prayers to the Trinity through the intercession of Our Lady and the Spiritual Master. The questions in this section seek to guide the reader to deeper devotion, a strengthened will, and an enlightened intellect.

4. CONTEMPLATIO—Contemplate

Contemplation is a simple gaze of the mind toward Christ and the things of God. Aided by God's grace, you are raised above meditation to a place of resting with God in Truth. Contemplation is:

The enjoyable admiration of perceived truth.
—St. Augustine

Elevation of the mind resting on God.
—St. Bernard of Clairvaux

Simple intuition of divine truth that produces love.
—St. Thomas Aquinas

. . . nothing else than a close sharing between friends; it means taking time frequently to be alone with him who we know loves us.
—St. Teresa of Ávila

"When we pray, we speak to God; but when we read, God speaks to us."
—St. Jerome

THE DOUAY-RHEIMS TRANSLATION

The Douay-Rheims Bible is a scrupulously faithful translation into English of the Latin Vulgate Bible, which Saint Jerome (342–420 AD) translated into Latin *from the original languages.* The Vulgate quickly became the Bible universally used in the Latin Rite.

Saint Jerome, who was one of the four great Western Fathers of the Church, was a man raised up by God to translate the Holy Bible into the common Latin tongue of his day. He knew Latin and Greek perfectly; he also knew Hebrew and Aramaic nearly as well. He was 1500 years closer to the original languages than any scholar today, which makes him a much better judge of the exact meaning of any Greek or Hebrew word in the Scriptures. Besides being a towering linguistic genius, he was also a great saint, and he had access to ancient Hebrew and Greek manuscripts of the 2nd and 3rd centuries *which have since perished and are no longer available to scholars today.* St. Jerome's translation, moreover, was a careful, word-for-word rendering of the original texts into Latin.

The Latin Vulgate Bible, from St. Jerome, has been read and honored by the Western Church for *fifteen hundred years*! It was declared by the Council of Trent to be the official Latin version of the canonical Scriptures. Hear what the Sacred Council decreed: "Moreover, the same Holy Council . . . ordains and declares that the old Latin Vulgate Edition, which, in use for so many hundred years, had been approved by the Church, be in public lectures, disputations, sermons and expositions held as authentic, and that no one dare or presume under any pretext whatsoever to reject it." (Fourth Session, April 8, 1546). As Pope Pius XII stated in his 1943 encyclical letter *Divino Afflante Spiritu,* this means the Vulgate is "free from any error whatsoever in matters of faith and morals." And the Douay-Rheims Bible is *a faithful, word-for-word translation of the Latin Vulgate Bible of St. Jerome.*

The Latin Vulgate New Testament was translated into English by members of the English College, Douai, in 1582, predating the King James Version (commissioned 1604, first published 1611). The Old Testament portion that makes up the Douay-Rheims Bible was translated into two volumes in 1609 and 1610 in Reims, France. Thus, the *Douay-Rheims* Bible.

INTRODUCTION TO THE GOSPEL OF SAINT JOHN

Saint John the Evangelist is one of the twelve apostles. In the gospel that bears his name, he calls himself only the "Beloved Disciple" or the "disciple whom Jesus loved", and especially so when he demonstrates affective love for Our Lord: when leaning at his breast at the Last Supper (John 13:23); by standing at the foot of the Cross with Mary (John 19:26); when, at the good news of Mary Magdalene, he races with Peter to the empty tomb (John 20:2); when he tells Peter he recognizes Jesus on the shore of Galilee after the resurrection (John 21:7); when Peter, himself in intimate conversation with Jesus on the shore of Galilee, asks about John's fate (John 21:20). The author of the fourth gospel identifies himself as this very disciple in its second to last verse (John 21:24).

John is brother to James the Greater, and Jesus calls the brothers the "Sons of Thunder" no doubt due to their passionate temperament (Mark 3:17). The one who leans his head at the breast of Jesus is no wilting lily: with his brother, James, he leaves their father immediately at the calling of Jesus to become fishers of men (Matt. 4:21–22); John zealously tries to forbid a non-follower from performing exorcisms in Jesus's name (Luke 9:49–50); James and John want to call down fire from heaven against a Samaritan town that does not receive Jesus (Luke 9:51–56); at their mother's instigation, they declare boldly to Jesus that they can drink the chalice of his suffering (Matt. 20:20–28). With Peter and James, John is a witness to the Transfiguration (Matt. 17:1–13) and to the raising of Jairus's daughter (Mark 5:35–43); Jesus also draws these three men closer to himself during his agony in the garden of Gethsemane (Matt. 26:36–46). After Pentecost, John and Peter cure a lame man, are thrown into prison, and speak boldly to the Jewish authorities (Acts 3–4). For good reason does Saint Paul recognize John as one of the three "Pillars of the Church" (Gal. 2:9).

While Peter establishes the Church in Antioch and Rome, and Paul proclaims the Gospel in Asia, Greece, Spain, and Rome, John builds up the Christian community in Judea and Ephesus. In Ephesus, he takes care of the Blessed Virgin Mary until her assumption into heaven, just as Jesus commands him to do (John 19:26–27). From Ephesus, John writes his gospel and three short letters (1–3 John). These letters speak about moral problems and the coming antichrist. John is no doubt also confronting the rise of Gnosticism, a series of heresies built upon claims of secret knowledge (*gnosis*) that Jesus has left concerning himself, and to which only initiates have access. In response to this, John reminds us of Jesus's words: "When the Spirit of truth comes, he will guide you into all truth" (John 16:13). John's sojourn in Ephesus is not peaceful—the Roman authorities try to execute the Son of Thunder by plunging him in boiling oil. When this fails, they exile him to the island of Patmos, where he writes the book of Revelation.

John's legacy continues strongly in the early Church. He takes in as disciples Saints Ignatius of Antioch and Saint Polycarp; the latter, in turn, teaches Saint Irenaeus. John, perhaps because he stands boldly at the foot of the Cross, is the only apostle not to die a martyr's death. John, most likely the youngest of the apostles, dies around the year 100 AD, in his early nineties. In the antiphons for Lauds on John's feast day (December 27), we celebrate John as a virgin—the only male saint for whom the Church does this.[1] When we read John's gospel, we should understand its author as a man in whom intense zeal is yoked to chaste affection for our Lord Jesus and our Lady Mary. This powerful combination drives the engine of John's contemplation of the Word made Flesh, because it is the very character of Jesus Christ.

John's gospel is an act of contemplation of the character of Christ. Jesus speaks boldly, performs signs, and extends a hand of tender mercy. Action and contemplation come together in Christ Jesus. John models it for us in the very structure of the gospel: the first part, consisting of chapters 1–12, features a series of miraculous signs paired to meditative discourses; the second part, consisting of chapters 13–21, tells of Jesus's passion, death, and resurrection, while our Lord reveals the deep mystery of the Trinity at work. When we read John's gospel, we are reading the character of the Beloved Disciple, who, through a life of active contemplation, becomes like his Lord in every way possible.

—Rev. Peter A. Heasley, SThD

---

1 Antiphon 1: "John, the apostle and evangelist, a virgin chosen by the Lord, was loved by the Lord above the others" (*Ioánnes, apóstolus et evangelista, virgo est eléctus a Dómino, atque inter céteros magis diléctus*); Antiphon 2: "To the virgin John, Christ, dying on the cross, entrusted his virgin mother" (*Iste est Ioánnes, cui Christus in cruce Matrem Vírginem vírgini commendávit*). This fact of John's virtue may help explain the special place of the one hundred forty-four thousand male virgins mentioned in Revelation 14:1–5.

INTRODUCTION TO SAINT AUGUSTINE

Augustine of Hippo was born on November 13, 354 AD, as Aurelius Augustinus to a father, Patricius, and a mother, Monica, Roman citizens of Berber origin. He is North African, born in Thagaste (modern Algeria) and ascends the ranks of late Roman society through a career as a teacher of rhetoric in Carthage (modern Tunisia), Rome, and Milan (by then the capital of the Roman Empire). In Milan, Saint Ambrose becomes a spiritual father to Augustine; Augustine converts to Christianity, organizes a community life for himself and his friends, and after the death of his mother, Monica, returns to Africa. There, he is ordained a priest and then bishop of the city of Hippo (modern Algeria), which he shepherds until he dies on August 28, 430 AD.

In this brief summary of the saint's life, we may be tempted to take his path to holiness as a given. Instead, we should see the work of grace. Augustine, one of the thirty-seven Doctors of the Church, is called the *Doctor gratiae*, the "Doctor of Grace." His more than sixty known works and six to ten thousand sermons treat matters as far ranging as Scripture, music, free will, and the Trinity, and at the core of his teaching is the doctrine of grace. Man is free to attain to the things of God only by God's gift of grace. Augustine knows this truth with agonizing clarity in his own life; in his most famous work, the *Confessions*, he lays bare a pre-conversion life of sexual dissolution and an ambition for fame that leads him, despite his Christian mother's pleas, to adopt the Near Eastern cult of Manichaeism as his religion. From the age of seventeen, he dwells in open concubinage with a woman, and they raise a son, Adeodatus. Augustine abandons her for the sake of a promising marriage with a younger woman but converts, with his son, to Christianity at the prompting of God's grace. Augustine recognizes the free gift of faith that God has given him despite his sinfulness, a gift prepared through many years of unhappy careerism, which nevertheless leads him to Ambrose's embrace, and through the many tears of his sainted mother, Monica.

As a Christian layman, priest, and bishop, Augustine lives in community according to a monastic rule that he himself draws up (and which still serves Augustinian communities today). The strength of spiritual brotherhood lifts him during a priestly career filled with strife: the Visigoths sack Rome in 410 AD, prompting Augustine to write *City of God*; the Vandals lay siege to Hippo in 430 AD, when Augustine dies. All the while, heresy and schism threaten the Church from within. So much of Augustine's homilies, including those on John, are directed against the Donatists, a North African sect that claims one must be re-baptized to rejoin the ranks of the Christian faithful after apostasy. Augustine, truly the Doctor of Grace, teaches the power of "one baptism for the forgiveness of sins," as we profess in our Creed.

With John the Evangelist, we read a man whose intense zeal, joined to tender affection for our Lord, lifts him to the heights of contemplation during a life of Gospel toil and exile; with Augustine's commentary on John's gospel, we read a man who recognizes the power of God's grace to restore him from a life of sexual dissolution and vain ambition and to raise him, likewise, to the heights of contemplation during a life of service to a Church facing the end of civilization as he knows it. Wherever we are on the spectrum of saintly virtue, we can trust that the grace by which Jesus calls

John, and Ambrose begets Augustine, can be ours, for our time, by a prayerful and meditative reading, a *lectio divina*, of these two spiritual fathers together.

Rev. Peter A. Heasley, SThD
Feast of the Epiphany of Our Lord, 2025

"The Scriptures are shallow enough for a babe to come and drink without fear of drowning and deep enough for theologians to swim in without ever reaching the bottom."
—St. Jerome

PRAYER BEFORE READING SCRIPTURE

Prayer for Knowledge of Scripture

Lord God, let us keep your Scriptures in mind
and meditate on them day and night,
persevering in prayer, always on watch.
We beg you, Lord, to give us real knowledge of what we read,
and to show us not only how to understand it,
but how to put it into practice,
and to obtain spiritual gifts
enlightened by the teaching of the Holy Spirit,
through Jesus Christ our Lord,
whose power and glory will endure throughout all ages.
Amen.
—Origen (c. 185–254)

Prayer Before Meditation

My Lord and my God, I firmly believe that you are here; that you see me, that you hear me. I adore you with profound reverence; I beg your pardon for my sins, and the grace to make this time of prayer fruitful. My Immaculate Mother, Saint Joseph my father and lord, my guardian angel, intercede for me. Amen.

Prayer to the Holy Spirit

Come, O Holy Spirit, fill the hearts and minds of your faithful servants and inflame them with the fire of your Divine love.

LET US PRAY

O God, who by the inspiration of the Holy Spirit did instruct the hearts of your faithful servants, grant us in the same Spirit to discern what is right and enjoy his comfort for ever. Through our Lord Jesus Christ, who lives and reigns one God with you and the same Spirit, world without end. Amen.

LECTIO: JOHN 1:1–5

Subject: The Beginning of Contemplation

[1] In the beginning was the Word, and the Word was with God,
and the Word was God. [2] The same was in the beginning with
God. [3] **All things were made by him:** and without him was made
nothing that was made. [4] In him was life, and the life was the light
of men. [5] And the light shineth in darkness, and the darkness did
not comprehend it.

Reading with St. Augustine

Saint Augustine's method in preparing a homily is to engage in a dialogue with his inner self, where the Holy Spirit dwells. He continues this method in his preaching, during which he asks his congregation to search with him. A common motif in Augustine's commentaries is the prompt, "Ask your heart" (*Interroga cor tuum)* (Augustine, *Homilies on the Gospel of John 1–40*).

Augustine calls Saint John a "mountain" for having reached the heights of contemplation and having understood what he sees above all created things, God within Himself: This mountain "had soared above all the peaks of the earth, soared beyond all the plains of the air, soared beyond the dizzy heights of the stars, soared beyond all the choirs and legions of angels. For, unless he soared above and beyond all these created things, he would never reach the one *through whom all things were made* (John 1:3). You can only have a sense of all that he surpassed if you notice where he ended up" (*Homilies* 1.5).

Augustine invites us, whom God has made through His Word, to meditate with him as creatures: "The one through whom the angel was made is the one through whom the maggot too was made; but the angel's proper place is heaven, the maggot's proper place is earth. The one who created things also arranged them. If he had put a maggot in the sky, you would find fault, if he had wanted angels to be born of rotting meat, you would find fault—and yet that is just about what God does, and he is not to be faulted. For, all human beings born of flesh, what are they but maggots? And from maggots he makes angels." (*Homilies* 1.13).

MEDITATIO

John's Gospel begins not with earthly events but with eternity: "In the beginning was the Word." It lifts us immediately to contemplation, calling us beyond what we see and touch to the mystery of God. Augustine, in his homilies, begins slowly, savoring each word, just as we must. To meditate on John's opening verses is to step into the vastness of God's light while still walking in the shadows of this world.

It will be our greatest happiness in heaven to contemplate God in Himself: Father, Son, and Holy Spirit. Contemplation should not intimidate us on earth. Contemplation is to move beyond our imagination, beyond created things, as John does. It is a gift, one received more perfectly with greater practice, and we practice contemplation with trust, silence, and detachment.

The Son of God is the Father's contemplation of Himself. The Word made Flesh draws the light of this contemplation down to us ("He that seeth me seeth the Father also"; John 14:9). There is no fault in starting with the flesh and the imagination, then, in what we call meditation. Meditation is the reflection on spiritual things through words and images. To read Scripture prayerfully is to meditate. We may lose focus at times or be distracted; we should accept disturbances peacefully. Our prayer may feel dry and uninspired; we should continue, confident that God gives all prayer as a gift in the times and ways we need it. He will never disappoint us. Our desire to raise our hearts and minds to Him pleases God and prepares a place in heaven for us.

ORATIO

1. Let me look at the blank page. An empty canvas is daunting for every artist and writer. Before any part of creation is made—heaven, angels, earth, humans—God simply is. I gaze upon the blank page the way I imagine God sees the emptiness of creation before He speaks it into existence, with similar love for whatever I will write on the pages of this book that God has for everything He has made.

2. Let me speak with the Holy Spirit, Who dwells in me as His temple. I ask to rest upon Him the way the Father and the Son rest in each other's gaze. I listen to the conversation that Father, Son, and Holy Spirit are having within my heart. I now ask Them what brings light.

3. Let me look at whatever I have written. I see the letters as a collection of creatures I have made through the words I know, and I love the heavenly light the Word of God has poured into the world through those creatures of ink. I see what angelic things God can do with the lowly, and I thank Him for them.

CONTEMPLATIO

LECTIO: JOHN 1:6–18

Subject: Praying with Humility

**6 There was a man sent from God, whose name was John. 7 This
man came for a witness, to give testimony of the light, that all
men might believe through him. 8 He was not the light, but was
to give testimony of the light. 9 That was the true light, which
enlighteneth every man that cometh into this world. 10 He was
in the world, and the world was made by him, and the world
knew him not.**

11 He came unto his own, and his own received him not.
12 But as many as received him, he gave them power to be made
the sons of God, to them that believe in his name. 13 Who are
born, not of blood, nor of the will of the flesh, nor of the will
of man, but of God. 14 And the Word was made flesh, and dwelt
among us, (and we saw his glory, the glory as it were of the only
begotten of the Father,) full of grace and truth. 15 John beareth
witness of him, and crieth out, saying: This was he of whom I
spoke: He that shall come after me, is preferred before me: because
he was before me.

16 And of his fulness we all have received, and grace for grace.
17 For the law was given by Moses; grace and truth came by Jesus
Christ. 18 No man hath seen God at any time: the only begotten
Son who is in the bosom of the Father, he hath declared him.

Reading with St. Augustine

Jesus says that among those born of women, none is greater than John the Baptist (see Matt. 11:11). Augustine builds upon this: "Because Jesus was a man in such a way that God was hidden in him, a great man [John] was sent ahead of him; by [John's] witness, [Jesus] would be found to be more than a man." John, as the perfection of all prophets, makes his followers see what can only be found in Jesus, the fulfillment of all prophecy (*Homilies* 2.5).

Augustine acknowledges a conundrum: If the world is made by the Word, how do His own in the world not receive Him? And he answers by defining the world in John 1:10 as those who love the world before God (see *Homilies* 2.11).

Augustine: "You were blinded by dust, you are healed by dust; so flesh blinded you; flesh heals you. The soul, you see, had become fleshly-minded by giving its consent to fleshly-minded inclinations, and that is how the eye of the heart had been blinded" (*Homilies* 2.16).

MEDITATIO

John's Gospel first lifts us to contemplation, but now he brings us back to the world—the world of sin, longing, and redemption. We are introduced to John the Baptist, not in grandeur, but in humility. His greatness lies not in his own merits, but in his mission: to point to Christ, the Light. John's superiority to earlier prophets is to point to the Flesh of Jesus and see in it, with God-given faith, the Son of God. The great John points to Christ with an act of humility, "He that shall come after me, is preferred before me" (John 1:15).

John the Baptist is our model, as sinners, for receiving Christ. We are in the world, and we love the world to some degree. Humility is to love another more than ourselves, and we receive the creative Word when we act with humility.

We do not have to become angels to receive Christ. His Flesh is medicine for our flesh. Moses sees God through cloud and fire and radiates fire (see Ex. 34:30). When we meditate on the Word made Flesh, we become more perfect humans, in body, soul, and spirit. We should not be afraid of our sins when we pray and meditate. The immaculate Word of God is not afraid of taking on our nature and paying the price for our sins. He inspires us, as He has inspired the prophets of old, for the sake of making Himself known among us and from within us—not as a reward for past behavior. Not even John, with all his perfections, is justified in this way. It is an act of humility to let Christ dwell within us, and this humility purges us of sin and love for the world.

ORATIO

1. It is time to acknowledge, honestly and without fear, my sins and the limits of my love. Let me list the things I want from this world: success, love, comfort, acknowledgment, satisfaction, and so on.

2. Despite these worldly loves, God has drawn me to this moment of meditation. He wants to shape my heart and mind to receive His

Word. Let me list the times and ways in which God has pointed out Christ to me, those persons who have been John the Baptist for me.

3. Let me make an act of humility before God, acknowledging my complete dependence on Him, His primacy in the life of the world, and the many ways in which He has worked through my limitations and failures.

CONTEMPLATIO

LECTIO: JOHN 1:19–34

Subject: My Role in the Church

19 And this is the testimony of John, when the Jews sent from
Jerusalem priests and Levites to him, to ask him: Who art thou?
20 And he confessed, and did not deny: and he confessed: I am not
the Christ.

21 **And they asked him: What then? Art thou Elias? And**
he said: I am not. Art thou the prophet? And he answered: No.
22 They said therefore unto him: Who art thou, that we may give
an answer to them that sent us? What sayest thou of thyself? 23 He
said: *I am the voice of one crying in the wilderness, make straight the*
way of the Lord, as said the prophet Isaias. 24 And they that were
sent, were of the Pharisees. 25 And they asked him, and said to
him: Why then dost thou baptize, if thou be not Christ, nor Elias,
nor the prophet?

26 **John answered them, saying: I baptize with water; but**
there hath stood one in the midst of you, whom you know not.
27 **The same is he that shall come after me, who is preferred**
before me: the latchet of whose shoe I am not worthy to loose.
28 These things were done in Bethania, beyond the Jordan, where
John was baptizing. 29 The next day, John saw Jesus coming to
him, and he saith: Behold the Lamb of God, behold him who
taketh away the sin of the world. 30 This is he, of whom I said:
After me there cometh a man, who is preferred before me: because
he was before me.

31 And I knew him not, but that he may be made manifest in
Israel, therefore am I come baptizing with water. 32 And John gave
testimony, saying: I saw the Spirit coming down, as a dove from
heaven, and he remained upon him. 33 **And I knew him not; but**
he who sent me to baptize with water, said to me: He upon
whom thou shalt see the Spirit descending, and remaining
upon him, he it is that baptizeth with the Holy Ghost. 34 And I
saw, and I gave testimony, that this is the Son of God.

Reading with St. Augustine

The people ask John who he is by comparing him to Elijah. Jesus, too, says John is Elijah (see Matt. 11:14). Augustine explains that John plays the same role as Elijah: John is the forerunner of the

Christ Who comes in humility and Elijah the eventual forerunner of the mighty Christ Who comes to judge (see *Homilies* 4.6).

Augustine says that Jesus, Who through His birth and crucifixion makes Himself the way of humility, is also baptized because "humility had to be lived fully by him in every situation." In this way, we too should not disdain to accept the Baptism of the Lord (*Homilies* 4.13; 5.3).

Augustine goes on to distinguish John's baptism from the Baptism we receive in the Church. John baptizes by his own authority as a just man in order to prepare the way of the Lord. The disciples of Christ baptize not by their own authority but by Christ's authority, which they exercise through their ministry. Once this ministry is established, once the way is prepared, there is no more need for John's baptism (see *Homilies* 5.6, 15).

MEDITATIO

John the Baptist stands by the Jordan, a man with a singular role in God's unfolding plan. Crowds press around him, questioning, challenging, seeking. *"Who are you?"* they demand. He does not flinch but answers plainly, *"I am not the Christ."* Nor does he claim the mantle of Elijah or any other figure of greatness. John's humility is disarming; he knows who he is before God. He is the voice in the wilderness, the one sent to prepare the way for Another.

John's ministry flows from this clarity. He baptizes those who confess their sins, not as an end in itself but to make room in their hearts for Christ. The water of John's baptism points ahead to the grace-filled waters of sacramental Baptism, instituted by the Lamb of God Himself. When Jesus appears, John's purpose becomes sharper: *"Behold, the Lamb of God, who takes away the sin of the world!"* It is an extraordinary proclamation, made by a man who claims no worthiness to even unfasten Christ's sandal.

John's humility and clarity of purpose illuminate our own roles in the Church and society. We, too, are called to serve, whether as parents, teachers, workers, or lay apostolate. Each role carries both authority and responsibility, which must be exercised with humility. The priest acts *in persona Christi* at the altar; parents guide their children; workers fulfill their duties—all in the spirit of Christ's humility.

Even in the smallest tasks, we join the great mission of the Church. At Mass, we unite as the body to the head, offering the sacrifice of Christ to the Father. Like John, we must point beyond ourselves to the One who gives our roles their meaning: the Lamb of God, who makes all things new.

ORATIO

1. What roles do I play in the Church and in society—in other words, what are the various relationships I have to others before God? Let me list them and thank God for them.

2. Do I exercise my authority over others with humility? Do I exercise the authority God has given me in a balanced way? Do I lord it over others or act meekly in my roles?

3. John the Baptist understands he is working for a specific purpose and that One greater than he will come after. Do I work to make my children, my colleagues and peers, and those who follow me in other roles more successful than I am? This is the way of humility.

CONTEMPLATIO

LECTIO: JOHN 1:35–51

Subject: Seeking Knowledge in Christ

35 The next day again John stood, and two of his disciples. 36 And
beholding Jesus walking, he saith: Behold the Lamb of God.
37 And the two disciples heard him speak, and they followed Jesus. 38 And Jesus turning, and seeing them following him, saith
to them: What seek you? Who said to him: Rabbi, (which is to
say, being interpreted, Master,) where dwellest thou? 39 He saith
to them: Come and see. They came, and saw where he abode, and
they stayed with him that day: now it was about the tenth hour.
40 And Andrew, the brother of Simon Peter, was one of the two
who had heard of John, and followed him.

41 He findeth first his brother Simon, and saith to him: We
have found the Messias, which is, being interpreted, the Christ.
42 **And he brought him to Jesus. And Jesus looking upon him,
said: Thou art Simon the son of Jona: thou shalt be called
Cephas, which is interpreted Peter.** 43 On the following day, he
would go forth into Galilee, and he findeth Philip. And Jesus saith
to him: Follow me. 44 Now Philip was of Bethsaida, the city of
Andrew and Peter. 45 Philip findeth Nathanael, and saith to him:
We have found him of whom Moses in the law, and the prophets
did write, Jesus the son of Joseph of Nazareth.

46 And Nathanael said to him: Can any thing of good come
from Nazareth? Philip saith to him: Come and see. 47 Jesus saw
Nathanael coming to him: and he saith of him: Behold an Is-
raelite indeed, in whom there is no guile. 48 Nathanael saith to
him: Whence knowest thou me? Jesus answered, and said to him:
Before that Philip called thee, when thou wast under the fig tree,
I saw thee. 49 Nathanael answered him, and said: Rabbi, thou art
the Son of God, thou art the king of Israel. 50 Jesus answered, and
said to him: Because I said unto thee, I saw thee under the fig tree,
thou believest: greater things than these shalt thou see.

51 **And he saith to him: Amen, amen I say to you, you shall
see the heaven opened, and the angels of God ascending and
descending upon the Son of man.**

Reading with St. Augustine

Augustine says, "Do not look for Christ anywhere else, except where Christ wanted to be preached to you; and hold onto him in the way he wished to be preached to you—in that way, write him on your hearts" (*Homilies* 7.7).

Augustine asks whether it is a greater thing that Christ knows the name of Simon's father or that He changes Simon's name to Peter. By stating the name of Simon's father, Jona, Jesus reveals that He has predestined Simon among the saints. By giving Simon a new name, Peter, Jesus signifies the Church in its nature as a rock (*petra*) (see *Homilies* 7.14).

Augustine suggests that the vision Jesus promises to Nathanael of the "angels of God ascending and descending upon the Son of Man" also signifies the Church. It is a reference to the dream of Jacob (see Gen. 28:11–18), in which the patriarch falls asleep on a stone and sees a ladder to heaven. The ladder extends from the rock as knowledge of Christ rises from the Church (see *Homilies* 7.23).

MEDITATIO

The disciples of John the Baptist were seekers, hearts tuned to the promise of the Messiah. They had come to John for repentance and a path to God. In their search, the Son of God found them. Quietly, He walked toward them until John declared, *"Behold, the Lamb of God!"* Stirred, they followed Jesus, who turned to ask, *"What seek you?"* They answered, *"Where dwelleth thou?"* Their search and desire for communion with God had found its end in Christ. He had opened their eyes, and they followed to remain with Him.

As St. Augustine reflects, Christ finds us where He wills. To some, He appears in life's order and discipline; to others, in chaos or despair. Yet wherever He finds us, it is to invite us to stay with Him. The Church soars upward wherever Christ is found.

In Peter, the Church is the rock, firm and unshaken, the foundation of God's grace and Sacraments. With Nathanael, the Church is a ladder of contemplation, rooted in doctrine but ascending heavenward. When Nathanael encountered Jesus, he marveled at being seen under the fig tree. Jesus promised him greater things: *"You will see the heaven opened, and the angels of God ascending and descending upon the Son of man."* Nathanael's faith soared, his heart set on the ladder of divine ascent. Both Peter's stability and Nathanael's contemplative spirit are vital: the rock grounds us, the ladder lifts us.

Our ascent, however, is only possible with communion with Christ. Each step is grace; every rung is His gift. To pass Him is to invite danger, but to stay with Him is to find peace. Christ is a "wall of defense against all the attacks and all the subterfuges of the enemy," so we should not fear so long as we hew close to Christ on our ascent among the angels (see *Homilies* 7.7).

ORATIO

1. The Church is a Rock united in Peter. Simon Peter is an imperfect man who comes to great faith and eventually lays down his life for Christ. Let me meditate on the enduring stability of the Church over the past two thousand years, despite the faults of her members and leaders, and see what Christ sees in Simon, son of Jona.

2. There are many temptations these days to hear secret knowledge, conspiracy theories, and alternative messages to the Church's preaching. Have I succumbed to this, and if so, what have I really gained, and what damage has falling to these temptations caused me?

3. The Church does offer means of meditation. Let the vision of the angelic ladder raise my heart to heavenly things and nourish a desire to go deeper both into doctrine and into the unspeakable mysteries of God.

CONTEMPLATIO

LECTIO: JOHN 2:1–12

Subject: What Christ Has Come to Do

1 And the third day, there was a marriage in Cana of Galilee: and
the mother of Jesus was there. 2 And Jesus also was invited, and
his disciples, to the marriage. 3 **And the wine failing, the mother
of Jesus saith to him: They have no wine.** 4 **And Jesus saith to
her: Woman, what is that to me and to thee? my hour is not yet
come.** 5 His mother saith to the waiters: Whatsoever he shall say
to you, do ye.

6 **Now there were set there six waterpots of stone, according to the manner of the purifying of the Jews, containing two
or three measures apiece.** 7 **Jesus saith to them: Fill the waterpots with water. And they filled them up to the brim.** 8 **And Jesus saith to them: Draw out now, and carry to the chief steward
of the feast. And they carried it.** 9 **And when the chief steward
had tasted the water made wine, and knew not whence it was,
but the waiters knew who had drawn the water, the chief steward calleth the bridegroom,** 10 **And saith to him: Every man at
first setteth forth good wine, and when men have well drunk,
then that which is worse. But thou hast kept the good wine
until now.**

11 This beginning of miracles did Jesus in Cana of Galilee; and
manifested his glory, and his disciples believed in him. 12 After this
he went down to Capharnaum, he and his mother, and his brethren, and his disciples: and they remained there not many days.

Reading with St. Augustine

Augustine suggests that the miracle of turning water into wine is nothing new for God, Who turns the rain into grapevines every day. We should tremble at God's everyday miracles, we whom God makes from nothing. Augustine says that this sign shows what Christ is doing in us: filling our insipid and foolish minds with wisdom and the intoxicating flavor of faith (see *Homilies* 8.1, 3; 9.1).

The sign also points to Jesus's revealing the Trinity in the fulness of time. The water in the jars represents the Old Testament, which receives its flavor when we recognize Christ in it. The six jars represent the six ages of mankind (Adam, Noah, Abraham,

David, Judah, and John the Baptist). They hold two or three measures each: two, because humanity comes from two people (Adam and Eve); three, because God is Three (see *Homilies* 9.5, 9–17).

Regarding Mary's intervention, Augustine explains Jesus's response, "What is that to me and to thee? my hour is not yet come," by distinguishing His relationship to her both as her Creator and as her Son. In this miracle, Jesus is acting by divine power, as her Creator and her Lord (see *Homilies* 8.9).

MEDITATIO

The wedding feast at Cana is alive with celebration. Joy fills the air, yet an unexpected lack—no more wine—threatens to overshadow the day. Mary, with quiet confidence, turns to her Son. *"They have no wine,"* she says, her words both simple and profound. Jesus's response, *"My hour has not yet come,"* hints at something greater, yet Mary trusts. She instructs the servants: *"Whatsoever he shall say to you, do ye."*

At her request, Jesus acts. Water, drawn in humble obedience, is transformed into the finest wine. The miracle is subtle, almost hidden, yet it carries immense significance. John the Evangelist arranges the first half of his gospel, chapters 1–12, according to seven great signs, beginning with this one and concluding with the resurrection of Lazarus in John 11. The One Who creates the world in seven days has come to announce His salvation through seven signs. As St. Augustine says, we should look beyond the miracle itself to what it signifies; we should tremble at the power of our Creator at work all around us, at the miracle of our own existence. He has made us from nothing for the sake of His love.

Jesus's transformation of water into wine points to His greater mission: to fulfill and redeem creation. The wine is not just for the wedding feast; it foreshadows the hour of His Passion, when His blood will be poured out for humanity. At Cana, Jesus affirms God's unwavering commitment to His creation, to the union of man and woman, and to the salvation of their children.

Mary's role is a model for us all. She does not command but participates, offering her intercession and trust. Creation and salvation are God's work, but He invites us to share in it. At Cana, the Creator reveals His power not only to provide but to perfect, transforming the ordinary into the extraordinary. In this, we glimpse the depth of His love—a love that will culminate on the cross, where His hour finally comes.

ORATIO

1. I may have lived part of my life without knowing Christ. How did this world look to me then? What did I think of myself? How has knowing Christ given flavor and wisdom to my mind?

2. Let me meditate on the miracle of my own existence and on the marvels of creation.

3. Mary, the Mother of Jesus, gives us a model of intercession before the Lord. Let me think of the ways in which I have called upon her and thank her for her intercession. What has been my own attitude before God? Do I make demands or express selfish desire while saying "Thy will be done?"

CONTEMPLATIO

LECTIO: JOHN 2:13–25

Subject: What Matters before Christ

13 And the pasch of the Jews was at hand, and Jesus went up to Jerusalem. 14 And he found in the temple them that sold oxen and sheep and doves, and the changers of money sitting. 15 **And when he had made, as it were, a scourge of little cords, he drove them all out of the temple, the sheep also and the oxen, and the money of the changers he poured out, and the tables he overthrew.**

16 **And to them that sold doves he said: Take these things hence, and make not the house of my Father a house of traffic.** 17 And his disciples remembered, that it was written: The zeal of thy house hath eaten me up. 18 The Jews, therefore, answered, and said to him: What sign dost thou shew unto us, seeing thou dost these things? 19 Jesus answered, and said to them: Destroy this temple, and in three days I will raise it up. 20 **The Jews then said: Six and forty years was this temple in building; and wilt thou raise it up in three days?**

21 **But he spoke of the temple of his body.** 22 When therefore he was risen again from the dead, his disciples remembered, that he had said this, and they believed the scripture, and the word that Jesus had said. 23 Now when he was at Jerusalem, at the pasch, upon the festival day, many believed in his name, seeing his signs which he did. 24 But Jesus did not trust himself unto them, for that he knew all men, 25 And because he needed not that any should give testimony of man: for he knew what was in man.

Reading with St. Augustine

Augustine, like many of the Church Fathers, engages in what we call a typological reading of Scripture. He sees the figures, events, and numbers given in the Bible as types or symbols of the spiritual reality we enjoy as Christians. Here, the rope Jesus uses to drive out the sellers and moneychangers symbolizes our sins: "All of us braid a rope for ourselves with our sins" when, instead of confessing them, we cover our sins with other sins (*Homilies* 10.5).

For Augustine, the doves for sale represent the grace of the Holy Spirit, which cannot be sold. The oxen are the Scriptures, since the prophets and apostles who write them are oxen, as Saint

Paul says (see 1 Cor. 9:9–10); there are some who misinterpret the Scriptures in order to mislead the people (see *Homilies* 10.6–7).

John the Evangelist himself understands the temple as a sign of Christ's body. Augustine calculates the forty-six years of its reconstruction as the sum of the letters in the name Adam, the source of Jesus's Flesh. Furthermore, the four letters in Adam's name signify, in Greek, the cardinal points of the earth (*anatole*, "east," *dusis*, "west," *arktos*, "north," *mesemthria*, "south." Adam, in Hebrew, means "earth." See *Homilies* 10.12).

MEDITATIO

The temple courts are bustling with noise—animals bleating, coins clinking, and voices bartering. Amid the chaos, Jesus steps forward and looks at what has become of the dwelling place of God. Fashioning a whip from cords, He drives out the merchants and money changers. *"Take these things hence, and make not the house of my Father a house of traffic!"* His words ring out, cutting through the clamor. The temple, built as a dwelling for God's glory, has become a marketplace.

Jesus's righteous anger is not just about animals and coins; it's about hearts. As St. Augustine reflects, materialism creeps into every corner of life, even religion. The temple was meant to be a space where God's grace could dwell, not a place for material transactions. When we treat the things of God—grace, wisdom, and freedom—as commodities to acquire, we forget that they are gifts, given freely by a loving Creator.

Jesus's actions are not destruction but restoration. Like Adam, formed from clay to house the Spirit of God, the temple is a symbol of humanity itself. Sin marred that temple, beginning with Adam and Eve's grasping for knowledge. What was meant to be enjoyed as grace became a source of division and destruction. Jesus, the New Adam, comes to rebuild what was broken, to restore the temple of God's presence in humanity, but he must first drive away sin.

His body is the new temple, the dwelling place of the Spirit. Through His Passion and Resurrection, He invites us into this restored reality. We are not called to grasp or take but to receive and enjoy the gifts of God. In cleansing the temple, Jesus calls us to remember our purpose: to be a dwelling place for grace, a space prepared by God for communion with Him.

ORATIO

1. Let me imagine myself standing in the temple area as Jesus approaches. For what reason have I come to the temple today: to buy my salvation, to sell my insight to others in the form of spiritual pride and vanity, or to inhabit the place where the Spirit dwells? What is the expression on Jesus's face as He looks at me?

2. Let me bring to mind my parish church and the things I enjoy about it (its architecture, liturgy, music, and comforts). I thank God for these things. I ask Him what my faith life would be without them; what would remain?

3. Let me write down my goals for the guided meditation in this book.

CONTEMPLATIO

LECTIO: JOHN 3:1–21

Subject: Nicodemus and Pride

1 And there was a man of the Pharisees, named Nicodemus, a ruler of the Jews. 2 This man came to Jesus by night, and said to him: Rabbi, we know that thou art come a teacher from God; for no man can do these signs which thou dost, unless God be with him. 3 **Jesus answered, and said to him: Amen, amen I say to thee, unless a man be born again, he cannot see the kingdom of God.** 4 **Nicodemus saith to him: How can a man be born when he is old? can he enter a second time into his mother's womb, and be born again?** 5 **Jesus answered: Amen, amen I say to thee, unless a man be born again of water and the Holy Ghost, he cannot enter into the kingdom of God.**

6 **That which is born of the flesh, is flesh; and that which is born of the Spirit, is spirit.** 7 Wonder not, that I said to thee, you must be born again. 8 The Spirit breatheth where he will; and thou hearest his voice, but thou knowest not whence he cometh, and whither he goeth: so is every one that is born of the Spirit. 9 Nicodemus answered, and said to him: How can these things be done? 10 Jesus answered, and said to him: Art thou a master in Israel, and knowest not these things?

11 Amen, amen I say to thee, that we speak what we know, and we testify what we have seen, and you receive not our testimony. 12 If I have spoken to you earthly things, and you believe not; how will you believe, if I shall speak to you heavenly things? 13 **And no man hath ascended into heaven, but he that descended from heaven, the Son of man who is in heaven.** 14 And as Moses lifted up the serpent in the desert, so must the Son of man be lifted up: 15 That whosoever believeth in him, may not perish; but may have life everlasting.

16 For God so loved the world, as to give his only begotten Son; that whosoever believeth in him, may not perish, but may have life everlasting. 17 For God sent not his Son into the world, to judge the world, but that the world may be saved by him. 18 He that believeth in him is not judged. But he that doth not believe, is already judged: because he believeth not in the name of the only begotten Son of God. 19 **And this is the judgment: because the light is come into the world, and men loved darkness rather**

than the light: for their works were evil. [20] **For every one that doth evil hateth the light, and cometh not to the light, that his works may not be reproved.**

[21] But he that doth truth, cometh to the light, that his works may be made manifest, because they are done in God.

Reading with St. Augustine

Augustine reframes Jesus's conversation with Nicodemus about being born again in terms of spiritual pride. He uses the example of Ishmael: he is born from Hagar's womb, but he is truly Sarah's son. He is a symbol of pride, which is why Sarah casts him and Hagar out. He cannot be born again either physically or spiritually. But now Jesus is speaking to proud Nicodemus about being born again spiritually (see *Homilies* 12.4).

Jesus speaks to Nicodemus through an earthly image because only Jesus can clearly see what is spiritual. Only He has ascended, the One Who has come down from the spiritual realm of heaven. Augustine says that this is not a prohibition on discerning spiritual things but rather an invitation to ascend with Christ even while on earth (see *Homilies* 12.8).

"You have to hate the work you have done in yourself and love the work God has done in you," Augustine says. This means distinguishing two things: the human being God has made and the sinner the human being has made. We are judged by ourselves when we reject salvation in Christ (*Homilies* 12.12–13).

MEDITATIO

Nicodemus came by night, cloaked in shadows—not just of the evening, but of pride. He was a teacher of Israel, learned and respected. Yet before Jesus, he was as a child, unable to grasp the mystery of being *"born again."* His mind strained at the edges of reason. *"How can a man be born when he is old?"* he asked, entangled in earthly thinking.

St. Augustine sees pride as the root of Nicodemus's blindness. Like Ishmael, cast out for his arrogance toward Isaac, Nicodemus could not be reborn while clinging to pride (*Homilies* 12.4). Spiritual rebirth demands humility—a descent from self-made heights to receive what only God can give.

Jesus pressed deeper: *"Unless a man be born of water and the Holy Ghost, he cannot enter into the kingdom of God."* His words shattered Nicodemus's earthly certainties. Rebirth was not something he could control or accomplish—it was a gift.

"He that descended from heaven, the son of Man is in heaven," Jesus continued. Augustine explains this mystery: Christ descended in humility so that we, united with Him, might ascend even now (*Homilies* 12.8). To rise, we must first fall—into surrender, into trust.

"He that doth truth cometh to the light." The true judgment is self-made when we cling to our works as our own. Only when we see every good thing as God's work in us can we rise with Christ, leaving pride behind in the shadows.

ORATIO

1. Let me put myself in Nicodemus's place. There may be certain things of the spiritual life or points of Church teaching I do not understand because I pride myself on my accomplishments or my knowledge. Nicodemus visits Jesus by night so he can expose his ignorance without being seen. In the privacy of these pages, let me tell Jesus what I do not yet understand.

2. Like Christ on earth, the Church dwells also in heaven. Do I limit my understanding of the way the Church is ordered to the way this world is governed? Can I see heavenly reasons for what the Church does?

3. Let me list the accomplishments for which I am most proud. Have any of these been an occasion of sin for me? If so, can I detach myself from them for the sake of salvation?

CONTEMPLATIO

LECTIO: JOHN 3:22–36

Subject: Spiritual Purity

[22] After these things Jesus and his disciples came into the land of Judea: and there he abode with them, and baptized. [23] And John also was baptizing in Ennon near Salim; because there was much water there; and they came and were baptized. [24] For John was not yet cast into prison. [25] And there arose a question between some of John's disciples and the Jews concerning purification.

[26] And they came to John, and said to him: Rabbi, he that was with thee beyond the Jordan, to whom thou gavest testimony, behold he baptizeth, and all men come to him. [27] John answered and said: A man cannot receive any thing, unless it be given him from heaven. [28] You yourselves do bear me witness, that I said, I am not Christ, but that I am sent before him. [29] **He that hath the bride, is the bridegroom: but the friend of the bridegroom, who standeth and heareth him, rejoiceth with joy because of the bridegroom's voice. This my joy therefore is fulfilled.** [30] He must increase, but I must decrease.

[31] He that cometh from above, is above all. He that is of the earth, of the earth he is, and of the earth he speaketh. He that cometh from heaven, is above all. [32] And what he hath seen and heard, that he testifieth: and no man receiveth his testimony. [33] He that hath received his testimony, hath set to his seal that God is true. [34] For he whom God hath sent, speaketh the words of God: for God doth not give the Spirit by measure. [35] The Father loveth the Son: and he hath given all things into his hand.

[36] He that believeth in the Son, hath life everlasting; but he that believeth not the Son, shall not see life; but the wrath of God abideth on him.

Reading with St. Augustine

The humility of John the Baptist comes forward again, of which John himself speaks using the imagery of bride, bridegroom, and friend of the bridegroom. His position is that of friend of the bridegroom, and it would be adultery for the bride, the Church, to love John or any person in place of Christ (see *Homilies* 13.10).

For Augustine, the imagery of the Church as bride of Christ brings to mind Old Testament expressions of God's people as virgin daughter Zion (see Is. 37:22 and Lam. 2:13, for instance). Augustine says that "the whole Church is being called a virgin," no matter the state in life of her members, as married, widowed, or vowed celibates. John the Baptist protects with his humility what Augustine calls the Church's "virginity of the mind," which is integral faith, solid hope, and sincere love (*Homilies* 13.12).

John the Baptist rejoices that Christ has come to His bride; he says that his joy is fulfilled. This joy is to announce the Father's giving all things into the Son's hand. Augustine says, "When [God] was good enough to send his Son to us, we must not suppose that we were sent anything less than the Father. In sending the Son, the Father sends his other self." John is grateful to announce this and does not take anything more for himself (*Homilies* 14.3, 11).

MEDITATIO

The Jordan's banks stirred with murmurs of concern. John's followers, troubled, approached him: *"Rabbi, He who was with thee . . . He baptizeth, and all men come to Him."* They feared their teacher was being overshadowed. But John's eyes shone with joy, not envy.

"He that hath the bride is the bridegroom," he declared. *"But the friend of the bridegroom . . . rejoiceth greatly."* St. Augustine calls this moment a proclamation of *"the wedding feast of the soul"* (*Homilies* 13.10). The Church is the bride, Christ her only Spouse. John stood as a joyful witness, content to fade into the background. *"He must increase, and I must decrease."*

Augustine warns that no human being should ever stand in Christ's place. No religious leader, no spiritual program, no earthly ministry should overshadow the Bridegroom's voice. True humility means serving without seeking glory—announcing Christ, not ourselves.

John's humility guards what Augustine calls *"virginity of the mind and heart"* (*Homilies* 13.12). This spiritual purity weds the soul to God alone through unshakable faith, steadfast hope, and sincere love.

"The Father loveth the Son, and hath given all things into His hand." John knew that the One to whom all divinity was given had come. His mission was complete—not diminished but fulfilled. His joy was made perfect, for the Bridegroom had arrived.

ORATIO

1. What is my state in life—married, widowed, single, in religious vows? Do I stand with John and herald Christ in this state of life?

Let me imagine with courage what doing so would look like in the specific details of my life and write down all that I would like to do to announce Christ.

2. How do I imagine my place in the Church? Can I let that image decrease for the sake of letting Christ increase in me?

3. The Church is the bride of Christ, the Son Who shares fully in God. If I have reduced my vision of Christ and the Church to anything less, let the Holy Spirit, Whom God gives without measure, bring the joy of this vision to greater fulness.

CONTEMPLATIO

LECTIO: JOHN 4:1–15

Subject: The Weakness of Christ for Salvation

1 When Jesus therefore understood that the Pharisees had heard
that Jesus maketh more disciples, and baptizeth more than John,
2 (Though Jesus himself did not baptize, but his disciples,) 3 He
left Judea, and went again into Galilee. 4 And he was of necessity
to pass through Samaria. 5 He cometh therefore to a city of Samaria, which is called Sichar, near the land which Jacob gave to
his son Joseph.

6 Now Jacob's well was there. **Jesus therefore being wearied**
with his journey, sat thus on the well. It was about the sixth
hour. 7 There cometh a woman of Samaria, to draw water. Je-
sus saith to her: Give me to drink. 8 For his disciples were gone
into the city to buy meats. 9 Then that Samaritan woman saith to
him: How dost thou, being a Jew, ask of me to drink, who am a
Samaritan woman? For the Jews do not communicate with the
Samaritans. 10 Jesus answered, and said to her: If thou didst know
the gift of God, and who he is that saith to thee, Give me to drink;
thou perhaps wouldst have asked of him, and he would have given
thee living water.

11 The woman saith to him: Sir, thou hast nothing wherein
to draw, and the well is deep; from whence then hast thou living
water? 12 Art thou greater than our father Jacob, who gave us the
well, and drank thereof himself, and his children, and his cattle?
13 Jesus answered, and said to her: Whosoever drinketh of this
water, shall thirst again; but he that shall drink of the water that I
will give him, shall not thirst for ever: 14 But the water that I will
give him, shall become in him a fountain of water, springing up
into life everlasting. 15 The woman saith to him: Sir, give me this
water, that I may not thirst, nor come hither to draw.

Reading with St. Augustine

Augustine focuses first on the weakness of Christ in this scene. He is weary from a journey. "The strength of Christ created you, the weakness of Christ recreated you," Augustine says. He compares Christ and the Samaritan woman in this moment to the creation of Adam and Eve. Eve is made not from flesh but from bone, from Adam's strength. "The woman was made, as it were, strong in the rib; Adam was made as it were weak in the flesh. It is Christ and the Church; his weakness is our strength" (*Homilies* 15.6–8).

This encounter with a woman at a well occurs at the sixth hour because it is the sixth age of the world, Augustine says (see Reflection on John 2:1–12). The Samaritan woman, a foreigner to Jews, is a type of the Church. "So then, let us listen to ourselves in her and recognize ourselves in her, and in her give thanks to God for ourselves" (*Homilies* 15.9–10).

MEDITATIO

The midday sun blazed as Jesus, weary from His journey, sat by Jacob's well. Thirst burned within Him, but His mission pressed deeper than water. As St. Augustine reflects, *"The strength of Christ created you; the weakness of Christ recreated you"* (*Homilies* 15.6). In His weariness, He revealed not defeat but an invitation—an opening for grace.

The Samaritan woman approached, expecting only silence—or scorn—from a Jewish man. Instead, Jesus spoke: *"Give Me to drink."* The request startled her. Why would He ask her, a Samaritan, for anything? Yet in His humble need, He placed Himself within her reach, offering her a place of rest.

Before we consider the sinfulness of the Samaritan woman, we should reflect on the weakness of Christ. This is Augustine's method. Before we accuse ourselves of the same sins as this person, we should see ourselves in the Samaritan woman, who prefigures the Church that Christ has come to save. This, indeed, is Christ's way.

Only after she desired what only He could give did He reveal her broken past. He made Himself weak so that His strength might save—not overwhelm—her. And in His humility, her thirst for life began.

ORATIO

1. This is a good moment to reflect on the order of my spiritual life. What occurs to me first, my sinfulness or Christ's weakness in saving me? Do I have to prove myself to God by becoming a sinless person? What message do I hear first from the Christians I know, that of sinfulness, or that of salvation?

2. Where has Christ been weak for me? I can gaze upon the Cross, but where has He borne the Cross in my life? In my own physical, emotional, or spiritual weakness? In the weakness of another for whom I care? In frustrating or desperate situations? Where has He met me in such a way that His strength does not intimidate me?

CONTEMPLATIO

LECTIO: JOHN 4:16–42

Subject: Exposing My Sins to Christ

16 Jesus saith to her: Go, call thy husband, and come hither.
17 The woman answered, and said: I have no husband. Jesus
said to her: Thou hast said well, I have no husband: 18 For thou
hast had five husbands: and he whom thou now hast, is not thy
husband. This thou hast said truly. 19 The woman saith to him:
Sir, I perceive that thou art a prophet. 20 Our fathers adored on
this mountain, and you say, that at Jerusalem is the place where
men must adore.

21 Jesus saith to her: Woman, believe me, that the hour cometh, when you shall neither on this mountain, nor in Jerusalem,
adore the Father. 22 You adore that which you know not: we adore
that which we know; for salvation is of the Jews. 23 But the hour
cometh, and now is, when the true adorers shall adore the Father
in spirit and in truth. For the Father also seeketh such to adore
him. 24 God is a spirit; and they that adore him, must adore him
in spirit and in truth. 25 The woman saith to him: I know that the
Messias cometh (who is called Christ); therefore, when he is come,
he will tell us all things.

26 Jesus saith to her: I am he, who am speaking with thee.
27 And immediately his disciples came; and they wondered that he
talked with the woman. Yet no man said: What seekest thou? or,
why talkest thou with her? 28 **The woman therefore left her wa-**
terpot, and went her way into the city, and saith to the men there:
29 Come, and see a man who has told me all things whatsoever I
have done. Is not he the Christ? 30 They went therefore out of the
city, and came unto him.

31 In the mean time the disciples prayed him, saying: Rabbi,
eat. 32 But he said to them: I have meat to eat, which you know
not. 33 The disciples therefore said one to another: Hath any man
brought him to eat? 34 Jesus saith to them: My meat is to do the
will of him that sent me, that I may perfect his work. 35 Do not
you say, There are yet four months, and then the harvest cometh?
Behold, I say to you, lift up your eyes, and see the countries; for
they are white already to harvest. 36 And he that reapeth receiveth
wages, and gathereth fruit unto life everlasting: that both he that
soweth, and he that reapeth, may rejoice together. 37 For in this is

the saying true: That it is one man that soweth, and it is another
that reapeth. [38] I have sent you to reap that in which you did not
labour: others have laboured, and you have entered into their la-
bours. [39] Now of that city many of the Samaritans believed in him,
for the word of the woman giving testimony: He told me all things
whatsoever I have done. [40] So when the Samaritans were come to
him, they desired that he would tarry there. And he abode there
two days.

[41] And many more believed in him because of his own word.
[42] And they said to the woman: We now believe, not for thy saying: for we ourselves have heard him, and know that this is indeed
the Saviour of the world.

Reading with St. Augustine

Augustine sees in the woman's five husbands our five senses: sight, sound, touch, taste, smell. The senses are husbands because they are "lawful partners, made by God and bestowed upon the soul by God." Our soul is subject to them until we fill it with intelligence and wisdom, which distinguish between what is good and evil among what our senses tell us (see *Homilies* 15.21).

The woman's bucket is lust, the well water is pleasure. No matter how much one draws, earthly pleasure never fully satisfies (see *Homilies* 15.16).

In the one with whom the woman is currently living, Augustine sees the figure of error. Error is an adulterer because it leads the intelligence into false ideas. In the case of this woman, these are false theological notions of Samaritan superiority over the Jews. But she calls Jesus a prophet: "The husband is beginning to come" (*Homilies* 15.22–23).

MEDITATIO

The Samaritan woman felt strangely at ease with Jesus. His weariness, His request for water—these small signs of human need broke the barrier between Jew and Samaritan, man and woman. In His humility, He had put Himself within her reach.

Then came His gentle truth: *"Go, call thy husband."* No accusation, just a simple statement that cut through pretense. *"I have no husband,"* she answered cautiously. *"Thou hast said well,"* Jesus replied, revealing her past without condemnation. He named her sins, but instead of despair, she felt relief.

St. Augustine reflects that Jesus did not scorn her questions or dismiss her as unworthy. He guided her deeper, turning her heart toward truth: He does not shun the questions of a sinner but draws her closer through conversation. Awakened, she spoke boldly: *"I perceive Thou art a prophet."* Her search for meaning collided with the reality of the Messiah standing before her.

Transformed, she abandoned her water jar—the symbol of earthly thirst—and ran back to her village. *"Come, see a man who told me all things whatsoever I have done,"* she exclaimed, her past now the key to proclaiming Christ's mercy.

Meanwhile, Jesus, being offered meat to eat and drawing on the woman's conversion, declared: *"My meat is to do the will of Him that sent Me."* In offering salvation, He drew strength. In humility, He brought life. In her, grace had begun its perfect work.

ORATIO

1. Let me sit in the Samaritan woman's place at the well. With what am I trying to fill my bucket? Where is Christ asking for a sip of water?

2. My five senses are a gift from God for living in this world. Have I given them over to the pleasures of food, drink, entertainments, sexuality, or other lusts? Have these lusts inspired bad ideas about God and the Church?

3. Many saints and modern-day public converts to Christianity speak openly of their past sins. They have encountered Christ without fear; with relief and joy, they call others to Christ by admitting how He has exposed their sins to them. Would I feel confident doing the same?

CONTEMPLATIO

LECTIO: JOHN 4:43–54

Subject: Reviving Faith

43 Now after two days, he departed thence, and went into Galilee. 44 **For Jesus himself gave testimony that a prophet hath no honour in his own country.** 45 And when he was come into Galilee, the Galileans received him, having seen all the things he had done at Jerusalem on the festival day; for they also went to the festival day.

46 He came again therefore into Cana of Galilee, where he made the water wine. And there was a certain ruler, whose son was sick at Capharnaum. 47 He having heard that Jesus was come from Judea into Galilee, went to him, and prayed him to come down, and heal his son; for he was at the point of death. 48 Jesus therefore said to him: Unless you see signs and wonders, you believe not. 49 The ruler saith to him: Lord, come down before that my son die. 50 Jesus saith to him: Go thy way; thy son liveth. The man believed the word which Jesus said to him, and went his way.

51 And as he was going down, his servants met him; and they brought word, saying, that his son lived. 52 He asked therefore of them the hour wherein he grew better. And they said to him: Yesterday, at the seventh hour, the fever left him. 53 **The father therefore knew, that it was at the same hour that Jesus said to him, Thy son liveth; and himself believed, and his whole house.** 54 This is again the second miracle that Jesus did, when he was come out of Judea into Galilee.

Reading with St. Augustine

This scene depicts the second of Jesus's signs (or wonders), which in Augustine's Latin are called *prodigia*: prodigies. Augustine takes us into the origin of this word, which means to "say or signify in advance." The wonders of God speak prophetically. In this case, the sign speaks about Jesus's ultimate rejection by His own people. Jesus has just spent two days among faith-filled Samaritans, and, back in His native Galilee, He chides the people for seeking signs in their faithlessness. Only the household of the child whom Christ heals comes to believe. "But because he founded *this* home country too, let him have honor here. He was rejected by the home country in which he was born; may he be received by the home country which he has caused to be born anew" (*Homilies* 16.1–7).

MEDITATIO

The royal official from Capharnaum pushed through the crowd, desperation driving him forward. His son was dying, and no Roman authority could help. He had heard of Jesus—a wonderworker, a healer. *"Come down before my child dies!"* he pleaded.

Jesus met his gaze—not with urgency, but with a challenge: *"Unless you see signs and wonders, you will not believe."* The words cut deep. The man's faith clung to the edge of sight and proof, but love for his son kept him from turning away. *"Sir, come,"* he begged again.

"Go, thy son liveth." No touch, no visible sign—just a word spoken in authority. The man believed and turned toward home, each step a quiet act of trust.

St. Augustine reflects that faith in signs is fragile, prone to fail when wonders cease. True faith holds fast to the Word, even when the eyes see nothing. In Augustine's age, the young Church battled heresies, struggling to teach the Faith amid fierce opposition. Their survival depended not on miracles but on trust in Christ's promises.

In our day, the Church in many places seems to lack the fervor it once had. Pews are emptying, churches are closing, parishes are merging, priests are becoming scarcer. We might hear of great evangelical strides made elsewhere and wonder what our faith should be asking for at home, where as among the Galileans, it seems to have grown cold. We can ask what it might take for Jesus to be born anew in our home.

ORATIO

1. Let me place myself among the Galileans who seek healing for the young boy. What do I want to see from Jesus? Is my zeal directed toward a moment's amazement, the restoration of a family, or the upheaval of all my comforts for the sake of bringing knowledge of Christ into the world?

2. In my *lectio divina*, have I yet encountered, or do I want to discover, anything new about Christ, anything strange or unfamiliar, where my faith might grow as among the Samaritans?

3. Let me pray to Jesus and ask Him in what way He wishes to be born anew in my heart, my home, and my church.

CONTEMPLATIO

LECTIO: JOHN 5:1–18

Subject: In God's Time

1 After these things was a festival day of the Jews, and Jesus went up to Jerusalem. 2 **Now there is at Jerusalem a pond, called Probatica, which in Hebrew is named Bethsaida, having five porches.** 3 In these lay a great multitude of sick, of blind, of lame, of withered; waiting for the moving of the water. 4 And an angel of the Lord descended at certain times into the pond; and the water was moved. And he that went down first into the pond after the motion of the water, was made whole, of whatsoever infirmity he lay under. 5 **And there was a certain man there, that had been eight and thirty years under his infirmity.**

6 Him when Jesus had seen lying, and knew that he had been now a long time, he saith to him: Wilt thou be made whole? 7 The infirm man answered him: Sir, I have no man, when the water is troubled, to put me into the pond. For whilst I am coming, another goeth down before me. 8 Jesus saith to him: Arise, take up thy bed, and walk. 9 And immediately the man was made whole: and he took up his bed, and walked. And it was the sabbath that day. 10 The Jews therefore said to him that was healed: It is the sabbath; it is not lawful for thee to take up thy bed.

11 He answered them: He that made me whole, he said to me, Take up thy bed, and walk. 12 They asked him therefore: Who is that man who said to thee, Take up thy bed, and walk? 13 But he who was healed, knew not who it was; for Jesus went aside from the multitude standing in the place. 14 Afterwards, Jesus findeth him in the temple, and saith to him: Behold thou art made whole: sin no more, lest some worse thing happen to thee. 15 The man went his way, and told the Jews, that it was Jesus who had made him whole.

16 **Therefore did the Jews persecute Jesus, because he did these things on the sabbath.** 17 **But Jesus answered them: My Father worketh until now; and I work.** 18 Hereupon therefore the Jews sought the more to kill him, because he did not only break the sabbath, but also said God was his Father, making himself equal to God.

Reading with St. Augustine

Augustine continues to see in the miracles of Jesus signs of the invisible reality Christ is bringing about. The pool and its water signify the Jewish people. Just as the pool has five porticos, God's chosen people have the five books of the Mosaic law. In the book of Revelation (or Apocolypse DR), John describes the many peoples as waters (see Apoc. 17:15). For Augustine, Jesus stirs up the peoples with His miracles and teaching (see *Homilies* 17.2–3).

The crippled man has been sick for thirty-eight years. Augustine does the math: forty is a number that signifies completion; what the man lacks is the twofold law of love for God and neighbor. When Jesus heals the man's infirmity, He supplies the grace of faith, hope, and love as well (see *Homilies* 17.6).

In response to those who persecute Jesus because He heals on the sabbath, Augustine invents a speech by Jesus: "Why do you expect me not to work on the sabbath? The sabbath day was enjoined upon you to signify *me*. You observe the works of God; I was there when they were done; all things were made through me; I know that. *My Father is working until now.* . . . My Father did not just work then when he made the world, he is also working now as he governs the world; accordingly, when he made the world, he made it through me; and as he governs it, he does so through me" (*Homilies* 17.15).

MEDITATIO

The paralytic lay by the pool of Bethesda, watching the water ripple as others hurried in, desperate for healing. Thirty-eight years he had waited, trapped in stillness while life surged past. *"I have no one to put me in the water,"* he muttered whenever hope stirred faintly within him.

Jesus approached—not with potions or formulas, but with presence. *"Wilt thou be made whole?"* His words were strange, almost piercing. Wasn't the answer obvious? Yet the question reached deeper than the body—it pierced the heart.

St. Augustine comments that Jesus's miracles are never random or transactional. They reveal who He is—the One who proceeds eternally from the Father—and who we are, spoken into being by His Word (*Homilies* 17.3). We are not created to live apart from Him; every healing is a call back into communion.

"Rise, take up thy bed, and walk." No water stirred, no hand lifted the man—only Christ's Word remade what was broken. Strength surged where none had existed. He walked—not just away from paralysis, but into a life forever marked by grace.

We, too, wait by life's troubled waters, longing for healing, for purpose. Jesus still asks: *"Wilt thou be made whole?"* He is not a distant dispenser of blessings but the One who makes us new, if only we rise at His command.

ORATIO

1. If I put myself at the pool of Bethsaida, leaning back against one of the pillars of its porticos, where do I feel Jesus is at this moment in my life?

2. If I were to list all the good things God has given me, could I also see how they have brought me closer to Him? Are there things that have not brought me closer to Him and to His Church?

3. The crippled man has waited nearly forty years for the healing he has wanted, and when he receives it, he becomes a witness to the divinity of Christ. Can I acknowledge the things God has withheld from me, the many times I've not been able to join the crowd in the stirring waters, and thank Him for holding back for a time?

CONTEMPLATIO

LECTIO: JOHN 5:19–29

Subject: Meditating on the Works of God

19 Then Jesus answered, and said to them: Amen, amen, I say unto you, the Son cannot do any thing of himself, but what he seeth the Father doing: for **what things soever he doth, these the Son also doth in like manner.** 20 For the Father loveth the Son, and sheweth him all things which himself doth: and greater works than these will he shew him, that you may wonder.

21 **For as the Father raiseth up the dead, and giveth life: so the Son also giveth life to whom he will.** 22 For neither doth the Father judge any man, but hath given all judgment to the Son. 23 That all men may honour the Son, as they honour the Father. He who honoureth not the Son, honoureth not the Father, who hath sent him. 24 Amen, amen I say unto you, that he who heareth my word, and believeth him that sent me, hath life everlasting; and cometh not into judgment, but is passed from death to life. 25 Amen, amen I say unto you, that the hour cometh, and now is, when the dead shall hear the voice of the Son of God, and they that hear shall live.

26 **For as the Father hath life in himself, so he hath given to the Son also to have life in himself:** 27 **And he hath given him power to do judgment, because he is the Son of man.** 28 **Wonder not at this; for the hour cometh, wherein all that are in the graves shall hear the voice of the Son of God.** 29 **And they that have done good things, shall come forth unto the resurrection of life; but they that have done evil, unto the resurrection of judgment.**

Reading with St. Augustine

We come to a perplexing discourse from Jesus, and Augustine tells us why our Lord speaks this way: to "disturb every twisted heart and exercise all the upright of heart." Jesus exercises our hearts to "clean them up, cleans them up to make them spacious, makes them spacious so as to fill them" (*Homilies* 21.1, 12).

Jesus, the Son, sees and does all that God the Father does. Jesus is the Word: "The Father said nothing which he did not say in the Son." God's being and His power are one; they are not separate, Augustine says. If the Son receives His being from the

Father, then He receives His power from the Father, too (*Homilies* 20.4; 21.4).

Jesus receives the power of life from the Father and exercises that power to raise us from the dead. Augustine speaks of two resurrections: a resurrection in the spirit now for those who believe and the resurrection of the flesh at the end of time (see *Homilies* 19.10, 16).

MEDITATIO

The crowds still buzzed with wonder at Jesus's miraculous healing of the paralytic at Bethesda. But now, in the stillness that followed, Jesus began to teach. *"The Son can do nothing of Himself, but what He seeth the Father doing."* His words opened a window into the inner life of God—a glimpse of the mystery the world had never seen but have been baptized into.

These signs are doorways to theology. Christ's works were not just displays of power but invitations to ponder the eternal relationship between Father, Son, and Spirit. Every healing, every miracle pointed beyond itself, revealing not only what God does but Who God is. We should not be afraid when something Jesus, or the apostles, or the prophets say perplexes us. As Augustine says, pondering such things is good exercise for our souls, and it frees us from fleshly thoughts.

"As the Father raiseth the dead and giveth life, so the Son also giveth life to whom He will." Jesus spoke not only of physical resurrection but of eternal life—new life for the soul even now. His words were both promise and judgment: *"The hour cometh . . . when all that are in the graves shall hear the voice of the Son of God."* Life and judgment rest in His hands.

ORATIO

1. Let me imagine standing on a beach. The water is endless and dangerously deep. The most I can enjoy of it is to stand in the lapping waves or to swim out a little. This is my share in the depths of God at the beginning of my prayer life.

2. The longer I stand before the ocean, the more keenly I will begin to feel its rhythms and discern its subtle movements: the tides, the currents, the life teeming within. This is the practice of meditation.

3. The resurrection is a promise of eternal life in our own bodies, which in the present order undergo death and decay. I imagine the day when Jesus returns to reorder all things toward life, and I, in this very body, can swim through the deepest ocean as I gaze upon the living God.

CONTEMPLATIO

LECTIO: JOHN 5:30–47

Subject: Measuring Myself to Christ

**[30] I cannot of myself do any thing. As I hear, so I judge: and my
judgment is just; because I seek not my own will, but the will
of him that sent me.**

[31] If I bear witness of myself, my witness is not true. [32] There
is another that beareth witness of me; and I know that the witness
which he witnesseth of me is true. [33] You sent to John, and he gave
testimony to the truth. [34] But I receive not testimony from man:
but I say these things, that you may be saved. [35] **He was a burning
and a shining light: and you were willing for a time to rejoice
in his light.**

[36] But I have a greater testimony than that of John: for the
works which the Father hath given me to perfect; the works themselves, which I do, give testimony of me, that the Father hath sent
me. [37] And the Father himself who hath sent me, hath given testimony of me: neither have you heard his voice at any time, nor
seen his shape. [38] And you have not his word abiding in you: for
whom he hath sent, him you believe not. [39] Search the scriptures,
for you think in them to have life everlasting; and the same are
they that give testimony of me. [40] And you will not come to me
that you may have life.

[41] I receive not glory from men. [42] But I know you, that you
have not the love of God in you. [43] I am come in the name of my
Father, and you receive me not: if another shall come in his own
name, him you will receive. [44] How can you believe, who receive
glory one from another: and the glory which is from God alone,
you do not seek? [45] Think not that I will accuse you to the Father.
There is one that accuseth you, Moses, in whom you trust.

[46] For if you did believe Moses, you would perhaps believe me
also; for he wrote of me. [47] But if you do not believe his writings,
how will you believe my words?

Reading with St. Augustine

In this deep discourse by our Lord Jesus, we hear about the life of God within Himself as a Trinity of persons and how that Trinity relates to us in terms of judgment. Augustine says that even though the Word is in the beginning with God, the Word is the

One to judge us because He is the Son of Man—that is, He is the One crucified in the Flesh for us (see *Homilies* 22.11).

Augustine follows this distinction into resurrection: God the Father resurrects souls, while the resurrection of the body comes about by the Son's humanity. Jesus takes Flesh in order to save us, body and soul. He Who has died and risen in the Flesh will judge us and raise our flesh from the dead (see *Homilies* 23.13).

To make it clearer what He means, Jesus returns to the example of John the Baptist, who bears witness to what Christ is saying. John is a lamp, and Augustine says that all human beings are lamps, which can be illuminated and put out, who either shine with the wisdom of the Holy Spirit or who burn out and stink (see *Homilies* 23.3).

MEDITATIO

Jesus continued to face His accusers, speaking not with anger but with certainty. *"I can do nothing of Myself . . . My judgment is just."* His voice resonated with authority rooted not in self-assertion, but in perfect obedience to the Father's will.

Jesus offers witnesses: *"The Father . . . John the Baptist . . . Moses."* Each testifies to His identity. John came as a burning, shining lamp, preparing hearts with fiery zeal. Moses wrote of Him, his law etched in stone but pointing toward the living Word. Yet, the clearest testimony was Christ's own works—the blind given sight, the dead raised, and sinners redeemed.

"If you did believe Moses, perhaps you would believe Me also." Jesus's words struck at hearts hardened against the fulfillment of Moses's teaching standing before them. Augustine emphasizes that Jesus will judge in human form—because what He has accomplished in the flesh is the standard to which He holds us. His humanity sanctifies ours, setting the standard for faith, hope, and love.

Our response matters. We are lamps meant to burn with His light, witnesses of His truth through works of faith, hope, and love. To believe is eternal life. To reject is judgment—not by a distant God, but by the One who lived, suffered, and rose, calling us to eternal life in body and soul.

ORATIO

1. John the Evangelist, who begins his gospel by contemplating the eternal life of God within Himself, recounts this discourse by Jesus in

order to draw me upward in prayer. Let me ascend with Him even if I cannot comprehend all that I see.

2. Jesus makes it easier to understand Him by pointing to John the Baptist and Moses as witnesses to His life and work. Which saints have helped me understand God?

3. Jesus will judge us and raise us as the Son of Man. By whose standards do I judge myself now? Do they match the work of Christ on earth?

CONTEMPLATIO

LECTIO: JOHN 6:1–15

Subject: Spending Time with What is Difficult

1 After these things Jesus went over the sea of Galilee, which is that of Tiberias. 2 And a great multitude followed him, because they saw the miracles which he did on them that were diseased. 3 Jesus therefore went up into a mountain, and there he sat with his disciples. 4 Now the pasch, the festival day of the Jews, was near at hand. 5 When Jesus therefore had lifted up his eyes, and seen that a very great multitude cometh to him, he said to Philip: Whence shall we buy bread, that these may eat?

6 And this he said to try him; for he himself knew what he would do. 7 Philip answered him: Two hundred pennyworth of bread is not sufficient for them, that every one may take a little. 8 One of his disciples, Andrew, the brother of Simon Peter, saith to him: 9 **There is a boy here that hath five barley loaves, and two fishes; but what are these among so many?** 10 Then Jesus said: Make the men sit down. Now there was much grass in the place. The men therefore sat down, in number about five thousand.

11 And Jesus took the loaves: and when he had given thanks, he distributed to them that were set down. In like manner also of the fishes, as much as they would. 12 And when they were filled, he said to his disciples: Gather up the fragments that remain, lest they be lost. 13 **They gathered up therefore, and filled twelve baskets with the fragments of the five barley loaves, which remained over and above to them that had eaten.** 14 Now those men, when they had seen what a miracle Jesus had done, said: This is of a truth the prophet, that is to come into the world. 15 Jesus therefore, when he knew that they would come to take him by force, and make him king, fled again into the mountain, himself alone.

Reading with St. Augustine

Augustine says, "Governing the whole cosmos . . . is a greater marvel than satisfying five thousand men on five loaves of bread." Jesus works this miracle, as His other miracles, to encourage our minds to rise to some understanding of God. God governs all things invisibly, and through a miracle like this, "We might even long to see in an invisible manner the one we recognized through things visible as invisible" (*Homilies* 24.1).

Again, Augustine finds in the numerology of the event an aid to our understanding the purpose of this miracle. The five loaves are the five books of Moses. They are made from barley, whose kernel is wrapped in a hard husk—like the truths of the Old Testament, which nourish us after great effort to unpack them. The two fish are the figures of the Old Testament priest and king—prefiguring the priest Who offers Himself as victim and the king Who rules us (see *Homilies* 24.5).

The twelve wicker baskets of leftovers are the mysterious truths that the crowd cannot grasp, which the Lord entrusts to the twelve apostles for their teaching (see *Homilies* 24.6).

MEDITATIO

Thousands had gathered, drawn by Jesus's words and signs, but now the sun dipped low, and need pressed upon them. *"Whence shall we buy bread, that these may eat?"* Jesus asked, testing His disciples.

Philip calculated the impossible. Andrew offered a boy's simple meal: five barley loaves and two fish—a laughable offering against such need. Yet Jesus took the humble gifts, lifted His eyes to heaven, and blessed them.

St. Augustine calls this moment a sign pointing beyond itself—a foretaste of the Eucharist. The bread, broken and shared, becomes more than food; it reveals Christ's life poured out. The crowd ate their fill, unaware they dined on a mystery far greater than multiplied loaves.

Like the loaves, Scripture itself is nourishment. Its "fleshly" images—priests, kings, prophets—are not relics of the past but living signs, revealing Christ when spiritually "broken open" and pondered. Nothing is wasted; even the twelve baskets of leftovers remind us that grace overflows.

As Passover approached, the true Bread of Life walked among them, unseen yet present. In every Eucharist, the visible and invisible meet: earthly bread, heavenly flesh. We, too, are called to recognize our Lord and offer right worship for what is humbly before us.

ORATIO

1. Augustine, like the other Church Fathers, is well-versed in the Old Testament. What Old Testament passages have most nourished my spiritual life?

2. Let me meditate on Old Testament passages that speak prophetically of the Eucharist, such as Gen. 14:18–20; Ex. 16:13–36; Ps. 22; Ps. 115.

3. Let me ruminate on an Old Testament passage that challenges or disturbs me, until I can taste what is spiritual in it.

CONTEMPLATIO

LECTIO: JOHN 6:16–40

SUBJECT: WHAT I SEEK AMIDST THE STORMS

16 And when evening was come, his disciples went down to the sea.
17 And when they had gone up into a ship, they went over the sea
to Capharnaum; **and it was now dark,** and Jesus was not come
unto them. 18 And the sea arose, by reason of a great wind that
blew. 19 When they had rowed therefore about five and twenty or
thirty furlongs, **they see Jesus walking upon the sea,** and drawing nigh to the ship, and they were afraid. 20 But he saith to them:
It is I; be not afraid.

21 They were willing therefore to take him into the ship; and
presently the ship was at the land to which they were going. 22 The
next day, the multitude that stood on the other side of the sea, saw
that there was no other ship there but one, and that Jesus had not
entered into the ship with his disciples, but that his disciples were
gone away alone. 23 But other ships came in from Tiberias; nigh unto
the place where they had eaten the bread, the Lord giving thanks.
24 When therefore the multitude saw that Jesus was not there, nor
his disciples, they took shipping, and came to Capharnaum, seeking
for Jesus. 25 And when they had found him on the other side of the
sea, they said to him: Rabbi, when camest thou hither?

26 Jesus answered them, and said: Amen, amen I say to you,
you seek me, not because you have seen miracles, but because you
did eat of the loaves, and were filled. 27 Labour not for the meat
which perisheth, but for that which endureth unto life everlasting,
which the Son of man will give you. **For him hath God, the Father, sealed.** 28 They said therefore unto him: What shall we do,
that we may work the works of God? 29 Jesus answered, and said
to them: This is the work of God, that you believe in him whom
he hath sent. 30 They said therefore to him: What sign therefore
dost thou shew, that we may see, and may believe thee? What dost
thou work?

31 Our fathers did eat manna in the desert, as it is written:
He gave them bread from heaven to eat. 32 Then Jesus said to them:
Amen, amen I say to you; Moses gave you not bread from heaven,
but my Father giveth you the true bread from heaven. 33 For the
bread of God is that which cometh down from heaven, and giveth
life to the world. 34 They said therefore unto him: Lord, give us

always this bread. [35] And Jesus said to them: I am the bread of life: **he that cometh to me shall not hunger: and he that believeth in me shall never thirst.**

[36] But I said unto you, that you also have seen me, and you believe not. [37] All that the Father giveth to me shall come to me; and him that cometh to me, I will not cast out. [38] Because I came down from heaven, not to do my own will, but the will of him that sent me. [39] Now this is the will of the Father who sent me: that of all that he hath given me, I should lose nothing; but should raise it up again in the last day. [40] And this is the will of my Father that sent me: that every one who seeth the Son, and believeth in him, may have life everlasting, and I will raise him up in the last day.

Reading with St. Augustine

Reflecting on the moment of Jesus's walking across the water, Augustine notes the detail John provides, that it was dark. He says, "As the end of the world approaches, errors increase, terrors multiply, wickedness spreads, infidelity increases. . . . The light is time and again extinguished; the darkness of hate among brothers spreads further day by day—and Jesus has not yet come. . . . And yet so great are the tribulations that even those who have come to believe in Jesus, and who are striving to persevere until the end, are terrified of falling away; though Christ is trampling on the waves, putting down the ambitious and the high-and-mighty of the world, Christians are terrified. Were not all these things foretold them?" (*Homilies* 25.5–7).

In the midst of all this, Christ becomes a sign that God has sealed. Augustine tells us that a seal marks what belongs to someone. Christ belongs to God. Christ appears to us in human form, and to set Him apart as special, God seals Christ for the Eucharist. Augustine gives words to Christ: "[God] has given me something that was mine, so that I would not be confused with the human race, but through me the human race will be freed" (*Homilies* 25.11).

Believing in the sign, then—eating the Eucharistic Bread—means believing in the one God has sealed. Augustine equates the expressions "he that cometh to me" with "he that believeth in me" and "shall not hunger" with "shall never thirst," that is, with spiritual thirst (see *Homilies* 25.13–14).

MEDITATIO

The waves crashed against the disciples' boat as they rowed through the darkened sea. The wind howled like an angry spirit, driving them far from shore. Exhausted and afraid, they strained against the storm—until a figure appeared, walking calmly on the waters.

"It is I; be not afraid." His voice cut through the chaos, steady as the hand that holds the deep. In that moment, the sea lost its power, and they were safe.

St. Augustine lived through storms of his own—empires collapsing, cities burning. The Roman world crumbled as waves of invaders surged across its lands. Yet Augustine saw beyond ruin. *"Christ walks upon the stormy sea,"* he preached, *"trampling down the proud."* He believed God was reshaping history, bringing new peoples into the fold, sealing their hearts with faith.

This same Christ comes to us, not just across turbulent seas but through the quiet miracle of the Eucharist. The Bread of Life, set apart by the Father, is given for every nation, race, and tongue. *"I am the bread of life,"* Jesus declared. *"He that cometh to Me shall not hunger."*

Faith in the Eucharist means trusting the One who still walks upon the troubled waters, commanding the storms of history and the tempests of the soul. In Him, we are never lost—only found, only fed, only saved.

ORATIO

1. Christ dies and rises so He can give me the Eucharist as my true spiritual food, food that sustains His faithful in their storm-tossed times. Can I imitate Christ and become food for the next generation of believers, even if they are different from me?

2. Augustine calls out the Christians of his day for being like the crowds who run after Christ for bread when He wants to give them Himself. What do I seek from the Church and my local community?

3. For what do I really hunger and thirst? If I say I want greater faith, do I still seek out fame, comfort, or some other material thing?

CONTEMPLATIO

LECTIO: JOHN 6:41–59

Subject: What the Eucharist Draws Together

[41] The Jews therefore murmured at him, because he had said: I am the living bread which came down from heaven. [42] And they said: Is not this Jesus, the son of Joseph, whose father and mother we know? How then saith he, I came down from heaven? [43] Jesus therefore answered, and said to them: Murmur not among yourselves. [44] **No man can come to me, except the Father, who hath sent me, draw him;** and I will raise him up in the last day. [45] **It is written in the prophets: *And they shall all be taught of God.* Every one that hath heard of the Father, and hath learned, cometh to me.**

[46] Not that any man hath seen the Father; but he who is of God, he hath seen the Father. [47] Amen, amen I say unto you: He that believeth in me, hath everlasting life. [48] I am the bread of life. [49] Your fathers did eat manna in the desert, and are dead. [50] This is the bread which cometh down from heaven; that if any man eat of it, he may not die.

[51] I am the living bread which came down from heaven. [52] If any man eat of this bread, he shall live for ever; and the bread that I will give, is my flesh, for the life of the world. [53] The Jews therefore strove among themselves, saying: How can this man give us his flesh to eat? [54] Then Jesus said to them: Amen, amen I say unto you: Except you eat the flesh of the Son of man, and drink his blood, you shall not have life in you. [55] He that eateth my flesh, and drinketh my blood, hath everlasting life: and I will raise him up in the last day.

[56] For my flesh is meat indeed: and my blood is drink indeed. [57] **He that eateth my flesh, and drinketh my blood, abideth in me, and I in him.** [58] As the living Father hath sent me, and I live by the Father; so he that eateth me, the same also shall live by me. [59] This is the bread that came down from heaven. Not as your fathers did eat manna, and are dead. He that eateth this bread, shall live for ever.

Reading with St. Augustine

Augustine lists several ways in which we are drawn to the Eucharist: by force, as when our unwilling children come to Mass; by pleasure, which the liturgy offers the heart and the mind; by real faith, when we seek Christ because He has God as His Father (see *Homilies* 26.2–5).

Being drawn by the Father to Christ is divine justice, Augustine says, the justice of God that makes us righteous. God's calling is a grace. We are not righteous without grace because we do not fulfill the law without grace. The law is love of God, and no one can love God except in the Holy Spirit, Whom Christ gives (see *Homilies* 26.1).

The Father draws us to Christ so that God Himself can teach us. This happens within the Church, which the Eucharist makes. Augustine says, "Thus by this food and drink he wishes that the fellowship of his body and members be grasped; that fellowship is the holy Church in his saints and his faithful, who have been predestined, and called, and justified, and glorified" (*Homilies* 26.7–9, 15).

MEDITATIO

The Jews murmured with disbelief. *"How can this man give us His flesh to eat?"* they asked, offended by Jesus's words. They saw only the son of Joseph, the carpenter's boy—but He spoke of bread from heaven, of life eternal.

"I am the living bread that came down from heaven," Jesus declared. *"He that eateth My flesh and drinketh My blood hath everlasting life."* His words cut through doubt, pointing beyond earthly understanding to the divine mystery of the Eucharist.

St. Augustine reflects that the Eucharist draws us not only to God but to one another. *"When you receive, you become,"* he teaches. In consuming Christ's Body and Blood, we are bound together as one Church, living members of His mystical Body. The Eucharist is not simply bread—it is the source of life, uniting us in God's love and justice.

We come to Mass drawn by memories of childhood faith, the comfort of familiar prayers, and the beauty of sacred song. Yet these are only the outer signs of a deeper reality: through the Eucharist, we stand before the Father, united in Christ's perfect offering.

It is within the wholeness of God's love for us and the Church He has made in Christ that we receive true knowledge. The Holy Spirit has moved the prophets, apostles, and saints throughout the ages to understand what God has set forth in Scripture and Tradition. Such insights can be ours when we come to God for no ulterior motive, under no constraint, but for love of being with God alone.

ORATIO

1. Let me lay out what has drawn me to prayer and liturgy from when I first began to know God. How have my motives changed?

2. Let me meditate on what connects the Eucharist to the Resurrection.

3. Let me take the courage to share something God has taught me with my family or faith community.

CONTEMPLATIO

LECTIO: JOHN 6:60–72

Subject: The Prudence of Christ

60 These things he said, teaching in the synagogue, in Capharnaum.
61 Many therefore of his disciples, hearing it, said: This saying
is hard; and who can hear it? 62 But Jesus, knowing in himself, that
his disciples murmured at this, said to them: Doth this scandalize
you? 63 If then you shall see the Son of man ascend up where he
was before? 64 **It is the spirit that quickeneth: the flesh profiteth
nothing. The words that I have spoken to you, are spirit and
life.** 65 But there are some of you that believe not. For Jesus knew
from the beginning, who they were that did not believe, and who
he was, that would betray him.
66 And he said: Therefore did I say to you, that no man can
come to me, unless it be given him by my Father. 67 After this
many of his disciples went back; and walked no more with him.
68 Then Jesus said to the twelve: Will you also go away? 69 And
Simon Peter answered him: Lord, to whom shall we go? thou
hast the words of eternal life. 70 And we have believed, and have
known, that thou art the Christ, the Son of God.
71 **Jesus answered them: Have not I chosen you twelve; and
one of you is a devil?** 72 **Now he meant Judas Iscariot, the son of
Simon: for this same was about to betray him, whereas he was
one of the twelve.**

Reading with St. Augustine

Augustine reflects often on where Christ is speaking from. He is among us in the Flesh, while He lives in the world of the spirit: "The Son of Man was in heaven in the same way as the Son of God was on earth; the Son of God on earth in the flesh he had taken, the Son of Man in heaven in the unity of the person." This explains Jesus's words in and about His Flesh as "spirit and life" (*Homilies* 27.4).

Augustine explains the words "the flesh profiteth nothing" by saying, "the flesh by itself." The flesh is useful the way a pen is useful for writing and the flesh of the apostles for preaching. The flesh on its own is lifeless, but when joined in the Spirit, even the flesh is life-giving (*Homilies* 27.5).

The only way to have life is to be joined to a living body; yet those, such as Judas, who though joined to the Body of Christ, dwell in spiritual death. According to Augustine, Jesus keeps Judas in His number for the sake of its perfection: the Twelve are sent to the four corners of the earth to proclaim the threefold God. God makes use even of evil because He can bring good from it (see *Homilies* 27.10).

MEDITATIO

The crowd responded, unsettled. *"This saying is hard; who can hear it?"* Many turned away, abandoning the One they had followed with such eagerness. Jesus's words about eating His flesh and drinking His blood were too much for them to hear.

Our Lord does not suffer regret as we do. He knows everything, including the one who will betray Him. He continues in His mission, despite what look like setbacks to us. Even in the Church, we tend to measure success in the flesh: numbers of converts and Mass-goers, an increase in the weekly collection, or school enrollment. The Son of Man sees what is spiritual, and He receives a spiritual response from Peter: "Thou hast the words of eternal life. And we have believed and have known, that thou art the Christ, the Son of God."

Turning to the Twelve, Jesus asked, *"Will you also go away?"* The question echoed with both challenge and invitation. Peter stepped forward, not with perfect understanding, but with unwavering trust: *"Lord, to whom shall we go? Thou hast the words of eternal life."* In that answer lay the Church's future—not built on human success, but on faith born of the Spirit.

Jesus did not praise Peter's response. *"One of you is a devil,"* He warned, forcing His disciples to reflect, just as they would at the Last Supper: *"Is it I, Lord?"* (Matt. 26:22).

The wisdom of Jesus's mission would be fully revealed at Pentecost, when these same apostles, filled with the Holy Spirit, would proclaim the mystery of the Eucharist to the world. Augustine calls them *"the pen of spiritual writing,"* their blood spilled in martyrdom the ink that would carry Christ's life-giving words to every generation. The Bread of Life had been broken—but not defeated. In His Body, the Church would rise.

ORATIO

1. Let me stand near Jesus at the end of His discourse. Let me pretend I know nothing of the Church's teaching on the Eucharist. How

do I respond to Jesus's words? How would they move me if I had heard them for the first time?

2. Jesus says His words are spirit and life. I am a person of flesh and bones, of earthly needs and desires. What does life mean for me? How do I define what is spiritual?

3. Still in Jesus's company, I have just heard my brother Peter confess his great faith in Christ. Jesus responds by saying one of us is a devil. Do I look for the traitor in order to protect our number, or do I accuse myself?

CONTEMPLATIO

LECTIO: JOHN 7:1–13

Subject: The Prudence of Christ

1 **After these things Jesus walked in Galilee; for he would not**
walk in Judea, because the Jews sought to kill him. 2 Now the
Jews' feast of tabernacles was at hand. 3 **And his brethren said to**
him: Pass from hence, and go into Judea; that thy disciples also
may see thy works which thou dost. 4 **For there is no man that**
doth any thing in secret, and he himself seeketh to be known
openly. If thou do these things, manifest thyself to the world.
5 **For neither did his brethren believe in him.**

6 **Then Jesus said to them: My time is not yet come; but**
your time is always ready. 7 The world cannot hate you; but me
it hateth: because I give testimony of it, that the works thereof are
evil. 8 Go you up to this festival day, but I go not up to this festival
day: because my time is not accomplished. 9 When he had said
these things, he himself stayed in Galilee. 10 **But after his brethren**
were gone up, then he also went up to the feast, not openly,
but, as it were, in secret.

11 The Jews therefore sought him on the festival day, and said:
Where is he? 12 And there was much murmuring among the multitude concerning him. For some said: He is a good man. And
others said: No, but he seduceth the people. 13 **Yet no man spoke**
openly of him, for fear of the Jews.

Reading with St. Augustine

Augustine says that Jesus decides to stay clear of Judea and instead go to Galilee so as to "console our frailty," not out of fear. He never ceases to be God and always has the power to go about wherever He wills (*Homilies* 28.1–2).

As with all the Church Fathers, Augustine identifies Jesus's brethren as His close relatives, especially Mary's nieces and nephews: "Just as no dead person had been in the tomb where the Lord's body was placed, either before or after, so neither did Mary's womb carry any mortal child either before or after." These cousins of His who want Him to perform miracles in Judea are "flesh talking to flesh," not knowing Jesus is Flesh—indeed, their flesh—united to God (*Homilies* 28.3–4).

Augustine reflects in two ways on Jesus's decision to go about in secret and the people's fear of speaking openly. Jesus says that while His time is not yet come, ours is always ready, so Augustine says, "Let the present, therefore, be the time for living justly; later on will come the time for judging those who have lived bad lives. . . . That will be the time for judgment." Augustine says this because the division between those who believe in Christ and those who think He "seduceth the people" holds even in Augustine's day (*Homilies* 28.6,12).

MEDITATIO

The Feast of Tabernacles drew near. Whispers of Jesus spread through the crowd—some in hope, others in hostility. His brothers urged Him to go publicly, to show His power through miracles. *"Manifest Thyself to the world,"* they insisted, their tone tinged with doubt.

But Jesus saw deeper. *"My time is not yet come,"* He replied calmly. *"Your time is always ready."* There is a time and a season for everything. He moved according to the will of the Father, guided by omniscient prudence.

St. Augustine reflects that Jesus's actions were as instructive as His words. He is like a skilled composer who knows when the music should rouse us and when it should draw us into meditation. The apostles would later follow His example: at times preaching openly despite persecution, at other times retreating or shaking the dust from their feet (Acts 13:51).

So, too, must the Church live. Sometimes she rises prominently in society, shaping culture and law; other times she moves in the shadows, her voice whispered in secret gatherings. We, too, are called to discern. Counsel is the better part of prudence. In our daily lives, we must ask the Holy Spirit when to speak boldly—and when to wait in silent trust, knowing that Christ's hour always comes.

ORATIO

1. Let me follow Jesus in this moment, as He goes about quietly. Am I like His family, who want Him to manifest Himself openly, to bring swift judgment on this world? Can I be patient with the injustice of this world?

2. Some people speak quite openly about their faith, while others keep quiet. What is my personality in this regard? Do I have gifts I am not sharing, or are there times I should be more prudent and reticent?

3. Am I aware of places the Church is currently operating underground, in secret, or in the face of persecution? What is my own situation?

CONTEMPLATIO

LECTIO: JOHN 7:14–36

Subject: Freedom in Selflessness

14 Now about the midst of the feast, Jesus went up into the temple,
and taught. 15 And the Jews wondered, saying: How doth this man
know letters, having never learned?

16 Jesus answered them, and said: My doctrine is not mine,
but his that sent me. 17 If any man will do the will of him; he shall
know of the doctrine, whether it be of God, or whether I speak of
myself. 18 **He that speaketh of himself, seeketh his own glory:
but he that seeketh the glory of him that sent him, he is true,
and there is no injustice in him.** 19 Did not Moses give you the
law, and yet none of you keepeth the law? 20 Why seek you to kill
me? The multitude answered, and said: Thou hast a devil; who
seeketh to kill thee?

21 Jesus answered, and said to them: One work I have done;
and you all wonder: 22 Therefore, Moses gave you circumcision,
(not because it is of Moses, but of the fathers;) and on the sabbath
day you circumcise a man. 23 If a man receive circumcision on
the sabbath day, that the law of Moses may not be broken; are
you angry at me because I have healed the whole man on the sabbath day? 24 **Judge not according to the appearance, but judge
just judgment.** 25 Some therefore of Jerusalem said: Is not this he
whom they seek to kill?

26 And behold, he speaketh openly, and they say nothing to
him. Have the rulers known for a truth, that this is the Christ?
27 But we know this man, whence he is: but when the Christ cometh, no man knoweth whence he is. 28 Jesus therefore cried out
in the temple, teaching, and saying: You both know me, and you
know whence I am: and I am not come of myself; but he that
sent me, is true, whom you know not. 29 I know him, because I
am from him, and he hath sent me. 30 They sought therefore to
apprehend him: and no man laid hands on him, because his hour
was not yet come.

31 But of the people many believed in him, and said: When
the Christ cometh, shall he do more miracles, than these which
this man doth? 32 The Pharisees heard the people murmuring these
things concerning him: and the rulers and Pharisees sent ministers
to apprehend him. 33 Jesus therefore said to them: Yet a little while

I am with you: and then I go to him that sent me. [34] You shall seek me, and shall not find me: and **where I am, thither you cannot come.** [35] The Jews therefore said among themselves: Whither will he go, that we shall not find him? will he go unto the dispersed among the Gentiles, and teach the Gentiles?

[36] What is this saying that he hath said: You shall seek me, and shall not find me; and where I am, you cannot come?

Reading with St. Augustine

Augustine returns to the theme of Christ's humility because John brings us back to that theme in this passage. Augustine challenges us who seek our own glory: "If Christ sought the glory of him that sent him, how much more should we be seeking the glory of him that made us?" On the contrary, the one who seeks his own glory, Augustine says, is called the Antichrist (*Homilies* 29.8).

John also brings us back to the theme of right judgment, so Augustine reflects: "This vice . . . is really hard to avoid in this world, not judging because of the person, but making right judgment." Jesus is speaking to the Jews of His day and to us in our day (*Homilies* 30.7).

Speaking of their day and ours, Jesus refers us to His day and hour. Augustine says that when Jesus returns in glory, we will also be set free from time; we will live in eternity. Jesus already lives there and says, "Where I am, thither you cannot come." Augustine clarifies: we cannot come *now*, but we will follow Jesus there when all space and time are fulfilled. Jesus is speaking of His resurrection and the general resurrection to come (see *Homilies* 30.9).

MEDITATIO

After a moment's retreat, Jesus returns to teaching and healing publicly. *"How does He know letters, having never learned?"* the scholars muttered, their judgment clouded by pride. Whispers rippled through the crowd: *"Is this not the One they seek to kill?"* Yet no hand moved against Him—His hour had not yet come.

St. Augustine reflects that Jesus's freedom came from His perfect obedience to the Father's will. He acted not from fear or ambition but from Truth itself. *"He that seeketh the glory of Him that sent Him, the same is true, and there is no injustice in Him."* Unlike the self-seeking rulers and fearful crowds, Jesus's purpose was singular: to reveal the Father.

The people could see Him, hear Him—but still could not grasp where He truly came from. *"You both know Me, and you know whence I am,"* He declared, *"but He that sent Me, is true, whom you know not."* Their judgments, bound by half-truths and assumptions, kept them blind.

Augustine warns that we are no different. Our limited understanding traps us in timid speculation, clinging to appearances. But those who seek God's glory are freed from human opinion and earthly gain.

When Christ returns, after all false kingdoms fall, those who lived for the Father's glory will reign with Him, body and soul. His resurrection is our promise: the more we seek God's glory now, the freer we act, because we are not bound to our own judgments or other people's opinions.

ORATIO

1. Let me stand in the temple area with Christ. Crowds of people are chattering on either side of me, speculating on Who Jesus is and what He will do next. Do I have the courage to speak up in this place?

2. When Jesus says, "Where I am, thither you cannot come," how do I feel? I could ask Him why, but let me think of other, sharper questions to ask Jesus: Where is He, and who do I need to be to join Him there?

3. Let me meditate on my own life and work. Are there parts of my goods and success I hold back for myself? Do I boast about my accomplishments? Am I trying to build a kingdom for myself in this world?

CONTEMPLATIO

LECTIO: JOHN 7:37–53

Subject: Unity in the Spirit

[37] And on the last, and great day of the festivity, Jesus stood and
cried, saying: If any man thirst, let him come to me, and drink.
[38] **He that believeth in me, as the scripture saith, *Out of his*
belly shall flow rivers of living water. [39] **Now this he said of the**
Spirit which they should receive, who believed in him: for as
yet the Spirit was not given, because Jesus was not yet glorified.
[40] Of that multitude therefore, when they had heard these words
of his, some said: This is the prophet indeed.
[41] Others said: This is the Christ. But some said: Doth the
Christ come out of Galilee? [42] Doth not the scripture say: That
Christ cometh of the seed of David, and from Bethlehem the
town where David was? [43] So there arose a dissension among the
people because of him. [44] And some of them would have appre-
hended him: but no man laid hands upon him. [45] The ministers
therefore came to the chief priests and the Pharisees. And they said
to them: Why have you not brought him?
[46] The ministers answered: Never did man speak like this
man. [47] The Pharisees therefore answered them: Are you also se-
duced? [48] Hath any one of the rulers believed in him, or of the
Pharisees? [49] But this multitude, that knoweth not the law, are
accursed. [50] Nicodemus said to them, (he that came to him by
night, who was one of them:)
[51] Doth our law judge any man, unless it first hear him, and
know what he doth? [52] They answered, and said to him: Art thou
also a Galilean? Search the scriptures, and see, that out of Galilee
a prophet riseth not. [53] And every man returned to his own house.

Reading with St. Augustine

Augustine distinguishes between our physical belly and our spiritual belly, the belly of the outer person, who seeks worldly things, and the belly of the inner person, who seeks spiritual things. "The belly of the inner person is the conscience of the heart," he says, and the water that flows from it is love for our neighbor (*Homilies* 32.4).

The living water is the Holy Spirit, who is love for God and for neighbor. This love is manifest, Augustine says, in the unity of charity. Augustine is defending the Catholic Church against heretics in his day, especially Donatists, Pelagians, and Sabellians. He says, "We have the Holy Spirit, if we love the Church" (*Homilies* 32.8).

Augustine notes that there are many people who have the Holy Spirit in a certain way before the Spirit is given to the whole Church at Pentecost: Simeon, Anna, and John the Baptist recognize Jesus; Zachariah and Mary speak boldly in the Holy Spirit before Jesus's birth, as have many prophets of old. The gift of the Spirit that is unique to the era of Christ's resurrection is unity in the Church toward eternal life in union with God, which is the Holy Spirit not just for a moment's prophecy, but His filling our inner belly for all eternity (see *Homilies* 32.6, 9).

MEDITATIO

Still in the temple, Jesus continued to teach, *"If any man thirst, let him come to Me and drink."* His words, clear and unnuanced, cutting through doubt and division. *"He that believeth in Me . . . out of his belly shall flow rivers of living water."* The crowd stirred, confused, some drawn in wonder, others hardened in suspicion.

St. Augustine sees this as a promise far greater than the people could grasp at that moment. Jesus spoke of the Holy Spirit, *"the spring of living water"* that would be poured out when He was glorified. This was no temporary refreshment, no earthly sign—it was the gift of divine love itself *until the end of the age.*

This Spirit, Augustine reminds us, is chiefly love for God and neighbor. Though the Spirit's gifts take many forms—wisdom, healing, prophecy—at its core is charity that unites us to God and one another. The living water flows only when we keep our hearts singularly focused on our Lord in reciprocating love.

The crowd that day could not yet understand. They debated His origin, His authority—missing the deeper call. But for those who thirsted truly, Jesus's words already stirred in their souls. In His coming Passion, the fountain would break open, and love would flow—healing, uniting, and transforming all who come to drink.

ORATIO

1. Let me stand before Christ and hear Him speak of springs of living water. Do I want to be such a spring for my neighbor?

2. Some in the Church seek special gifts or have received them without asking—gifts of tongues, of prophecy, of teaching, of healing, and so on. If I possess such a gift, do I use it for the purpose of Church unity?

3. Let me pray for unity in the Catholic Church and among all Christians.

CONTEMPLATIO

LECTIO: JOHN 8:1–11

Subject: Taking Our Shame to the Cross

1 **And Jesus went unto mount Olivet.** 2 And early in the morning he came again into the temple, and all the people came to him, and sitting down he taught them. 3 And the scribes and Pharisees bring unto him a woman taken in adultery: and they set her in the midst, 4 And said to him: Master, this woman was even now taken in adultery. 5 Now Moses in the law commanded us to stone such a one. But what sayest thou?

6 **And this they said tempting him, that they might accuse him.** But Jesus bowing himself down, wrote with his finger on the ground. 7 **When therefore they continued asking him, he lifted up himself, and said to them: He that is without sin among you, let him first cast a stone at her.** 8 **And again stooping down, he wrote on the ground.** 9 **But they hearing this, went out one by one, beginning at the eldest. And Jesus alone remained, and the woman standing in the midst.** 10 Then Jesus lifting up himself, said to her: Woman, where are they that accused thee? Hath no man condemned thee?

11 Who said: No man, Lord. And Jesus said: Neither will I condemn thee. Go, and now sin no more.

Reading with St. Augustine

Augustine sees the Mount of Olives as a kind of arena for Jesus. People are anointed with olive oil, and Christ means "one who is anointed." He has also anointed us like athletes in the arena: "He has made us wrestlers against the devil" (*Homilies* 33.3).

Anointed in the Spirit, Jesus possesses the qualities of truth, meekness, and justice (Augustine refers to Psalm 44:5). Those with whom Jesus contends recognize the truth of His words and the meekness of His manner, so in the arena of Mount Olivet, His enemies try to trap Him in justice: the law says a woman must be stoned for adultery (see *Homilies* 33.4).

Augustine shows how the scribes and Pharisees fall into the very trap they have set for Jesus: "Outwardly, you see, they were lying; inwardly, they failed to examine themselves; they were looking at the adulteress, they had no eyes for themselves. While transgressing the law, they were eager for the law to be carried out" (*Homilies* 33.5).

MEDITATIO

The morning sun climbed above the temple as a mob pushed a woman into the courtyard, their voices sharp with accusation. *"Master, this woman was taken in adultery . . . Moses commanded us to stone such a one."* They stood ready, stones in hand, certain of their own righteousness.

Jesus stooped, tracing silently in the dust, unmoved by their clamor. Then He rose, His gaze steady. *"He that is without sin among you, let him first cast a stone at her."* The words struck harder than any rock, exposing hearts bound by hidden guilt. Augustine has a brilliant insight into the woman's response to Jesus's words. The woman is waiting for sinless Jesus to cast that stone. She is more terrified than ever.

The humility of confessing our sins while not judging others is hard work. That is why Augustine likens it to a wrestling match. How often do we have to pin down our tongue to keep it from uttering judgment! And we try to slip our way out of the accuser's grasp when our sin weakens us.

Jesus does condemn the sin, but not the sinner. How does He separate the sin from the sinner? He neither allows us to live how we please nor leads us into the despair of never being forgiven. Jesus makes us gaze upon His Cross, which is our salvation as well as the standard of our judgment. It is the wellspring of divine love, the love without which we cannot live. Jesus takes this woman's sins to the Cross; His justice reaches perfection in love. He has anointed us for the same purpose.

ORATIO

1. Jesus brings the adulterous woman's sins to the Cross to save her. He commands us to take up our cross daily and follow Him. Are there persons I need to forgive, whose sins I must let hang on the cross of my heart?

2. An examination of conscience can reveal to us sins of which we may not be aware and help us, in the Holy Spirit, to trace their source and effects. Do I make a daily examination of conscience?

3. It can be hard to forgive ourselves, too, and to let go of sins even after sacramental confession. Shame is a strong force. Jesus despises the shame of the Cross (see Heb. 12:2)—in other words, He hangs in utter humiliation, knowing that He is accomplishing something greater than overcoming the shame of sin. When I gaze upon the Cross, can I, too, let go of shame for the sake of embracing the joy of my Savior's forgiveness?

CONTEMPLATIO

LECTIO: JOHN 8:12–30

Subject: The Cross as Revelation

12 Again therefore, Jesus spoke to them, saying: I am the light of
the world: he that followeth me, walketh not in darkness, but shall
have the light of life. 13 The Pharisees therefore said to him: Thou
givest testimony of thyself: thy testimony is not true. 14 Jesus answered, and said to them: Although I give testimony of myself,
my testimony is true: for I know whence I came, and whither I go:
but you know not whence I come, or whither I go. 15 You judge
according to the flesh: I judge not any man.

16 And if I do judge, my judgment is true: because I am not
alone, but I and the Father that sent me. 17 And in your law it is
written, that the testimony of two men is true. 18 I am one that
give testimony of myself: and the Father that sent me giveth testimony of me. 19 They said therefore to him: Where is thy Father?
Jesus answered: Neither me do you know, nor my Father: if you
did know me, perhaps you would know my Father also. 20 These
words Jesus spoke in the treasury, teaching in the temple: and no
man laid hands on him, because his hour was not yet come.

21 Again therefore Jesus said to them: I go, and you shall seek
me, and you shall die in your sin. Whither I go, you cannot come.
22 The Jews therefore said: Will he kill himself, because he said:
Whither I go, you cannot come? 23 **And he said to them: You are
from beneath, I am from above. You are of this world, I am not
of this world.** 24 Therefore I said to you, that you shall die in your
sins. For if you believe not that I am he, you shall die in your sin.
25 They said therefore to him: Who art thou? Jesus said to them:
The beginning, who also speak unto you.

26 Many things I have to speak and to judge of you. But he
that sent me, is true: and the things I have heard of him, these
same I speak in the world. 27 And they understood not, that he
called God his Father. 28 **Jesus therefore said to them: When you
shall have lifted up the Son of man, then shall you know, that I
am he, and that I do nothing of myself, but as the Father hath
taught me, these things I speak:** 29 And he that sent me, is with
me, and he hath not left me alone: for I do always the things that
please him. 30 When he spoke these things, many believed in him.

Reading with St. Augustine

The emperor Constantine prohibits crucifixion in AD 337; Augustine explains that this is not just to honor Christ but also to keep criminals from being honored by dying in the same manner as the Lord. The Cross is the way in which the people of Jesus's day judge Him according to the flesh, but Jesus bears with this in order to make the Cross an instrument of His mercy. The Cross is now the measure of spiritual judgment, to which the Father and the Spirit bear witness: "There you have him even as judge; but acknowledge him as savior, so as not to experience the judge" (*Homilies* 36.4–5).

When Jesus speaks of the Son of Man being lifted up, Augustine identifies this with the Cross, not His ascension. The Cross is the place from which we understand Jesus's relationship to God the Father (see *Homilies* 40.2). Jesus has chosen the hour and demonstrates complete power of dying and living, condemning and forgiving (see *Homilies* 37.9). This power makes Him judge (see *Homilies* 36.11).

We, therefore, should raise our eyes upward, to the place from which Jesus, even while on earth, exercises the power to judge—above heaven, to the Father Himself. Following the standard of our judgment, the Cross, upward transforms us into those whom He will judge favorably: "Accept Christ as from above, so that you may soar in thought beyond everything that has been made, beyond absolutely the whole of creation, every material body, every created spirit, everything which is in any way at all subject to change; yes, soar above it all, just as John did, so that he might reach and touch *In the beginning was the Word, and the Word was with God, and the Word was God* (John 1:1)" (*Homilies* 38.4).

MEDITATIO

As the woman's accusers retreated in anger or shame, Jesus turned to the gathered crowd. His voice rose with clarity and command: *"I am the light of the world: he that followeth Me walketh not in darkness, but shall have the light of life."* The Jews again murmured, their eyes still clouded with earthly concerns.

"Whither I go, you cannot come." His words pierced through their shallow judgments, calling them to something beyond appearances. St. Augustine reflects that Jesus was raising their gaze toward the only path that could reach Him—*"the way of the Cross"*. They judged Him wrongly by human standards, but He would transform the Cross, their instrument of condemnation, into the bridge to eternal life.

"When you shall have lifted up the Son of Man, then shall you know that I am He." In this lifting, the Crucified would become the Judge—not by power seized, but by mercy poured out. The Cross would become the standard of perfect love, the doorway through which all must pass.

It is only at the Cross, standing shoulder to shoulder with John the Evangelist, that our souls can soar to spiritual heights. At the Cross, Jesus shows that all judgment based on sensory appearances is futile; He exercises spiritual power over flesh. At the Cross, Jesus reveals Himself as Creator with the Father of all things, including the world of the spirit, the world in which we find true life. Acknowledging Jesus as Lord is our act of faith in our movement toward communion with the Father.

ORATIO

1. It may not seem obvious to us how judgment impedes our faith. We judge by appearances, while faith is a gift from God. Let me call to mind for what things in the world spiritual faith has been a light.

2. There are situations we acknowledge as sinful and people we know potentially at risk of eternal death. Without judgment, I commend them to the mercy of the Cross and am at peace.

3. John the Evangelist wants us to soar with him on eagle wings of contemplation. Judgment is a act of the intellect joined to our material senses. Contemplation is a spiritual act. Let me gaze upon the Cross and meditate on the power over all creation Jesus exercises as Lord.

CONTEMPLATIO

LECTIO: JOHN 8:31–47

Subject: Jesus's Tough Love

31 Then Jesus said to those Jews, who believed him: If you continue in my word, you shall be my disciples indeed. 32 And you shall know the truth, and the truth shall make you free. 33 **They answered him: We are the seed of Abraham, and we have never been slaves to any man: how sayest thou: you shall be free? 34 Jesus answered them: Amen, amen I say unto you: that whosoever committeth sin, is the servant of sin.** 35 Now the servant abideth not in the house for ever; but the son abideth for ever.

36 If therefore the son shall make you free, you shall be free indeed. 37 **I know that you are the children of Abraham:** but you seek to kill me, because my word hath no place in you. 38 I speak that which I have seen with my Father: and you do the things that you have seen with your father. 39 **They answered, and said to him: Abraham is our father. Jesus saith to them: If you be the children of Abraham, do the works of Abraham. 40 But now you seek to kill me, a man who have spoken the truth to you, which I have heard of God. This Abraham did not.**

41 **You do the works of your father. They said therefore to him: We are not born of fornication: we have one Father, even God.** 42 Jesus therefore said to them: If God were your Father, you would indeed love me. For from God I proceeded, and came; for I came not of myself, but he sent me: 43 Why do you not know my speech? Because you cannot hear my word. 44 **You are of your father the devil, and the desires of your father you will do. He was a murderer from the beginning, and he stood not in the truth; because truth is not in him. When he speaketh a lie, he speaketh of his own: for he is a liar, and the father thereof. 45 But if I say the truth, you believe me not.**

46 Which of you shall convince me of sin? If I say the truth to you, why do you not believe me? 47 He that is of God, heareth the words of God. Therefore you hear them not, because you are not of God.

Reading with St. Augustine

"The first freedom is to be without serious sin," Augustine says. He then repeats John the Evangelist's affirmation that no one is without sin, at least small ones (see 1 Jn. 1:8). Serious sin is worthy of condemnation (*Homilies* 41.9–10).

In Augustine's day, a slave who suffers under a bad master has the right to be sold to another one who will treat him better. A slave of sin has no recourse but to enslave himself to Christ, Who is Truth: "Let us ask to be put up for sale, to be redeemed by his blood" (*Homilies* 41.4).

Jesus recognizes that the Jews are children of Abraham, but when He calls them to imitate Abraham, they turn from claiming Abraham as their father to claiming God as their Father. But Jesus calls them out on this, stating instead that their father is the devil because they will do to Jesus what the devil did to Adam: lie and murder Him (see *Homilies* 42.5–7).

MEDITATIO

This long and important discourse turns from matters of right judgment and faith to sin and freedom. Jesus is speaking to "those Jews, who believed him." *"If you continue in My word, you shall be My disciples indeed . . . and the truth shall make you free."* His voice was steady, but His words struck deeply.

St. Augustine reflects that Jesus spoke not to wound but to shape them—*like a carpenter shaping wood,* sawing and sanding with harsh truths. True freedom is not lawless choice but living bound to Christ through love and obedience. Slavery to sin is easy; freedom in Christ requires discipline, reflection, and a transformed heart.

Jesus's next words were sharper still: *"You are of your father the devil."* He spoke to break their false security, calling them to renounce sin's deceit and become true children of God. *"If God were your Father, you would love Me."*

Augustine reminds us that to enslave oneself to Christ is to be free. Bound by His Blood, we become God's family—spiritually descendants of Abraham, bonded in truth and love. Sin separates, but Christ's Word unites. In Him, truth is not just known—it makes us free to live fully.

To enslave oneself to Christ is to live in the freedom of the truth. Freedom is not choice to do whatever we want. We are bound to God and to each other by Christ's Blood. To be bound by blood is a relationship of family—of being children of God and of Abraham, spiritually and in the way of covenant. We imitate the saints with whom we live unless, through serious sin, we leave our Father's house and take up with bad friends and false fathers.

ORATIO

1. We are children of God through faith, adopted at Baptism and conformed through Confirmation and the Eucharist. Children always grow restless in their parents' house. Where do I still seek false freedoms in the world?

2. Have I ever felt a harsh word from Jesus in prayer or through a neighbor—has anyone called me out on hypocrisy, sin, or selfishness? Has this word re-created me in the image of a freeborn child of God or made me bitter?

CONTEMPLATIO

LECTIO: JOHN 8:48–59

Subject: Testing Our Heart

48 **The Jews therefore answered, and said to him: Do not we
say well that thou art a Samaritan, and hast a devil?** 49 **Jesus
answered: I have not a devil:** but I honour my Father, and you
have dishonoured me. 50 But I seek not my own glory: there is one
that seeketh and judgeth.

51 Amen, amen I say to you: If any man keep my word, he
shall not see death for ever. 52 The Jews therefore said: Now we
know that thou hast a devil. Abraham is dead, and the prophets;
and thou sayest: If any man keep my word, he shall not taste death
for ever. 53 Art thou greater than our father Abraham, who is dead?
and the prophets are dead. Whom dost thou make thyself? 54 Jesus
answered: If I glorify myself, my glory is nothing. It is my Father
that glorifieth me, of whom you say that he is your God. 55 And
you have not known him, but I know him. And if I shall say that
I know him not, I shall be like to you, a liar. But I do know him,
and do keep his word.

56 **Abraham your father rejoiced that he might see my day:
he saw it, and was glad.** 57 The Jews therefore said to him: Thou
art not yet fifty years old, and hast thou seen Abraham? 58 Jesus
said to them: Amen, amen I say to you, before Abraham was
made, I am. 59 They took up stones therefore to cast at him. But
Jesus hid himself, and went out of the temple.

Reading with St. Augustine

Augustine notes that Jesus denies having a devil but He does not deny being a Samaritan. Jesus does not return curse for curse, insult for insult, but He does make a distinction. Augustine points out that "Samaritan" (from the Hebrew *shamar*) means guardian; Jesus is our guardian, as He illustrates in the parable about Himself as the Good Samaritan (see Luke 10:25–37) (see *Homilies* 43.2).

Augustine distinguishes two sorts of temptation: one that deceives and one that tests. This whole exchange, going back to the beginning of John 7, has been a sort of test to reveal the inner quality of those with whom Jesus has been speaking. Augustine gives the example of Job: "Job was hidden from himself but not from God, who gave permission to the tempter and let [Job] know himself" (*Homilies* 43.6).

Jesus Himself gives the example of Abraham, who sees and rejoices in Jesus as "God abiding with the Father, due to come in the flesh at a certain time without ever leaving the bosom of the Father." In other words, faith gives Abraham eyes to see, while still in the flesh, the One Who will come in the Flesh without leaving heaven (*Homilies* 43.16).

MEDITATIO

The culmination of Jesus's discourse in John 8 reaches its apex when He declares, "Before Abraham was made, I am." With these words, Jesus reveals His divinity, echoing the name of God revealed to Moses at the burning bush. This profound statement is both an invitation to faith and a mirror that reveals the hearts of His listeners. Those who once claimed belief in Him now call Him possessed and prepare to stone Him, their hearts hardened against the truth.

Revelation often comes as a test, not just of belief but of the soul's readiness to see itself as it truly is. The call to faith in God challenges our reliance on material senses and earthly judgments. Jesus asks His audience to consider Abraham's faith, a faith that looked beyond the seen to trust in the unseen. Similarly, knowing God requires a willingness to face our own sinfulness and to embrace both the mercy we receive and the mercy we must give.

Jesus hides Himself at the end of this episode, and once again, this is not because He cannot withstand whatever stones they want to throw at Him but because it is prudent for Jesus to achieve His purpose for these people: faith in Him when He dies and rises from the dead. But we must be careful when Jesus reveals us to ourselves, Augustine warns: "As a man he fled from stones, but woe to those from whose hearts of stone God fled!" (*Homilies* 43.17).

ORATIO

1. Jesus does not trade insult for insult, but turns the trade of words into a way to deepen knowledge of Him and His audience. How do I engage with those who disagree with me?

2. It may happen that God has allowed me to enter very trying situations like Abraham and Job. How has my knowledge of God and myself deepened through them? Does any part of my heart remain cased in stone?

CONTEMPLATIO

LECTIO: JOHN 9:1–17

Subject: Now Is the Time for Good

1 **And Jesus passing by, saw a man, who was blind from his birth.** 2 And his disciples asked him: Rabbi, who hath sinned, this man, or his parents, that he should be born blind? 3 Jesus answered: Neither hath this man sinned, nor his parents; but that the works of God should be made manifest in him. 4 **I must work the works of him that sent me, whilst it is day: the night cometh, when no man can work.** 5 **As long as I am in the world, I am the light of the world.**

6 **When he had said these things, he spat on the ground, and made clay of the spittle, and spread the clay upon his eyes,** 7 And said to him: Go, wash in the pool of Siloe, which is interpreted, Sent. He went therefore, and washed, and he came seeing. 8 The neighbours therefore, and they who had seen him before that he was a beggar, said: Is not this he that sat and begged? Some said: This is he. 9 But others said: No, but he is like him. But he said: I am he. 10 They said therefore to him: How were thy eyes opened?

11 He answered: That man that is called Jesus made clay, and anointed my eyes, and said to me: Go to the pool of Siloe, and wash. And I went, I washed, and I see. 12 And they said to him: Where is he? He saith: I know not. 13 They bring him that had been blind to the Pharisees. 14 Now it was the sabbath, when Jesus made the clay, and opened his eyes. 15 Again therefore the Pharisees asked him, how he had received his sight. But he said to them: He put clay upon my eyes: and I washed, and I see.

16 Some therefore of the Pharisees said: This man is not of God, who keepeth not the sabbath. But others said: How can a man that is a sinner do such miracles? And there was a division among them. 17 They say therefore to the blind man again: What sayest thou of him that hath opened thy eyes? And he said: He is a prophet.

Reading with St. Augustine

For Augustine, the man born blind stands in for all humanity, struck blind in spirit by the sin of Adam (see *Homilies* 44.1).

Christ smears the blind man's eyes with clay to demonstrate the stages of Christian initiation. The catechumen, the one learning the Faith, has been anointed but has not yet been washed in Baptism. The mixture of spittle and clay is, according to Augustine, "the Word made Flesh," the union of divinity and humanity by which we learn about God and are washed to behold His light (*Homilies* 44.2).

Jesus speaks about day and night. Day is the time when Christ and the Church are working in the world and in our lives. Night is the end of time and the end of our lives, "when no one can work but can only receive what he has accomplished," Augustine says (*Homilies* 44.6).

MEDITATIO

The sun shone brightly as Jesus and His disciples walked past a man born blind, huddled near the temple gate. His milky eyes stared into darkness, untouched by light since birth. The disciples, eager for theological insight, asked, *"Rabbi, who hath sinned, this man, or his parents, that he should be born blind?"*

Jesus stopped, His gaze steady. *"Neither hath this man sinned, nor his parents: but that the works of God should be made manifest in him."* His words swept aside the logic of blame, revealing a deeper mystery. This man's suffering was not punishment—it was purpose. Somehow it belonged in God's plan for salvation.

We can trace Jesus's affirmation back to the sin of our first parents. *O felix culpa, quae talem ac tantum meruit habere Redemptorem*, we sing in the Exultet at the Easter Vigil, "O happy fault that earned for us so great, so glorious a redeemer." God permits evil, even moral evil such as that committed by Adam and Eve and many others around us, for the sake of the great good God brings out of it. Original sin and the varied circumstances of our life often leave us in darkness, but the work of Christ as the Word of God is our guiding light until unending day. This is a profound call to trust.

ORATIO

1. Have I experienced a loss I cannot trace to my own action? Even if I could, can I wash in the clay of Christ's humanity, hung upon the Cross for me, and see the situation in light of the good Christ's divinity will provide?

2. There will come a moment when we can no longer build up and perfect our works of faith, hope, and love, the night of judgment that leads to the day of resurrection for the just. Are there works of mercy I could do now that I am putting off?

CONTEMPLATIO

LECTIO: JOHN 9:18–41

Subject: Judging Right Religion

[18] The Jews then did not believe concerning him, that he had been blind, and had received his sight, until they called the parents of him that had received his sight, [19] And asked them, saying: Is this your son, who you say was born blind? How then doth he now see? [20] His parents answered them, and said: We know that this is our son, and that he was born blind:

[21] **But how he now seeth, we know not; or who hath opened his eyes, we know not: ask himself: he is of age, let him speak for himself.** [22] **These things his parents said, because they feared the Jews: for the Jews had already agreed among themselves, that if any man should confess him to be Christ, he should be put out of the synagogue.** [23] Therefore did his parents say: He is of age, ask himself. [24] They therefore called the man again that had been blind, and said to him: Give glory to God. We know that this man is a sinner. [25] He said therefore to them: If he be a sinner, I know not: one thing I know, that whereas I was blind, now I see.

[26] They said then to him: What did he to thee? How did he open thy eyes? [27] He answered them: I have told you already, and you have heard: why would you hear it again? will you also become his disciples? [28] They reviled him therefore, and said: Be thou his disciple; but we are the disciples of Moses. [29] We know that God spoke to Moses: but as to this man, we know not from whence he is. [30] The man answered, and said to them: Why, herein is a wonderful thing, that you know not from whence he is, and he hath opened my eyes.

[31] Now we know that God doth not hear sinners: but if a man be a server of God, and doth his will, him he heareth. [32] From the beginning of the world it hath not been heard, that any man hath opened the eyes of one born blind. [33] Unless this man were of God, he could not do anything. [34] They answered, and said to him: Thou wast wholly born in sins, and dost thou teach us? **And they cast him out.** [35] Jesus heard that they had cast him out: And when he had found him, he said to him: Dost thou believe in the Son of God?

36 He answered, and said: Who is he, Lord, that I may believe in him? 37 And Jesus said to him: Thou hast both seen him; and it is he that talketh with thee. 38 **And he said: I believe, Lord. And falling down, he adored him.** 39 **And Jesus said: For judgment I am come into this world; that they who see not, may see; and they who see, may become blind.** 40 And some of the Pharisees, who were with him, heard: and they said unto him: Are we also blind?

41 Jesus said to them: If you were blind, you should not have sin: but now you say: We see. Your sin remaineth.

Reading with St. Augustine

John the Evangelist tells us the parents of the man born blind are afraid of the Jewish authorities, which is why they do not answer for their son. Augustine sees another motive in their saying "Ask himself: he is of age": they saw that it was no longer bad to be put out of the synagogue, that Christ was welcoming people (see *Homilies* 44.10).

Because he is thrown out of the synagogue, Augustine says, the man born blind becomes a Christian. The word Siloe or Siloam means "Sent": the man is now a prophet, sent by God to confess his faith (see *Homilies* 44.15).

As soon as the man confesses his faith to Jesus, Jesus says, "For judgment I am come into this world." Yet Jesus has already said, "I do not judge anyone" (John 8:15). In the light of Christ, we are to judge ourselves now, as faithful and seeing or proud and blind. This is the judgment about which Christ speaks here, when he says, "For judgment I am come." He will come again at the end of the world to judge the living and the dead, and that is not yet happening at his first coming, which is why Jesus says for us to hear, "I do not judge anyone" (John 8:15) (*Homilies*, 44.17).

MEDITATIO

The once-blind man stood alone before the furious Pharisees, their eyes blazing with contempt. They demanded explanations, dismissing his miracle as trickery or sin. *"Give glory to God,"* they sneered. *"We know that this Man is a sinner."*

St. Augustine reflects that spiritual blindness is far worse than physical darkness. The Pharisees' pride clouded their vision, chaining them to reject Christ. They clung to religious identity without faith, mistaking custom for righteousness. They cannot see what the formerly blind man sees.

Driven by anger, they cast the man out of the synagogue—an exile shared by early Christians like St. Paul. But he was not abandoned. Jesus sought him out, speaking gently: *"Dost thou believe in the Son of God?"*

"Who is He, Lord, that I may believe?" the man asked eagerly. *"Thou hast both seen Him, and it is He that talketh with thee."* Falling to his knees, he confessed: *"Lord, I believe."*

Augustine reminds us that true faith is not mere tradition or intellectual assent but a radical posture of humility before Christ. Only when we fall at His feet, confessing our need, can we see clearly—illuminated by the Light of the World.

ORATIO

1. The word "Siloe" or Siloam means "Sent." The man cured of his blindness becomes one sent to confess his faith in Christ Jesus. Have I shared with others the way or ways in which God has given me faith?

2. It is possible for a Christian to act proudly and blindly, like the authorities before the man born blind. What do I value most as a Christian? Do I see myself as distinct, better than others in the Church?

CONTEMPLATIO

LECTIO: JOHN 10:1–21

Subject: Through the Gate of Contemplation

1 Amen, amen I say to you: He that entereth not by the door into the sheepfold, but climbeth up another way, the same is a thief and a robber. 2 But he that entereth in by the door is the shepherd of the sheep. 3 **To him the porter openeth;** and the sheep hear his voice: and he calleth his own sheep by name, and leadeth them out. 4 And when he hath let out his own sheep, he goeth before them: and the sheep follow him, because they know his voice. 5 But a stranger they follow not, but fly from him, because they know not the voice of strangers.

6 This proverb Jesus spoke to them. But they understood not what he spoke to them. 7 **Jesus therefore said to them again: Amen, amen I say to you, I am the door of the sheep.** 8 All others, as many as have come, are thieves and robbers: and the sheep heard them not. 9 I am the door. By me, if any man enter in, he shall be saved: and he shall go in, and go out, and shall find pastures. 10 The thief cometh not, but for to steal, and to kill, and to destroy. I am come that they may have life, and may have it more abundantly.

11 I am the good shepherd. The good shepherd giveth his life for his sheep. 12 **But the hireling, and he that is not the shepherd, whose own the sheep are not, seeth the wolf coming, and leaveth the sheep, and flieth: and the wolf catcheth, and scattereth the sheep:** 13 **And the hireling flieth, because he is a hireling: and he hath no care for the sheep.** 14 I am the good shepherd; and I know mine, and mine know me. 15 As the Father knoweth me, and I know the Father: and I lay down my life for my sheep.

16 **And other sheep I have, that are not of this fold: them also I must bring, and they shall hear my voice, and there shall be one fold and one shepherd.** 17 Therefore doth the Father love me: because I lay down my life, that I may take it again. 18 No man taketh it away from me: but I lay it down of myself, and I have power to lay it down: and I have power to take it up again. This commandment have I received of my Father. 19 A dissension rose again among the Jews for these words. 20 And many of them said: He hath a devil, and is mad: why hear you him?

21 Others said: These are not the words of one that hath a
devil: Can a devil open the eyes of the blind?

Reading with St. Augustine

Augustine tells us how Jesus can declare Himself both the gate and the porter (gatekeeper): "Who, then, opens himself if not he who explains himself?" Augustine allows us to understand the Holy Spirit as the gatekeeper, too, since He teaches us all truth (*Homilies* 46.4).

The gate is open, and there are sheep on the outside who will come inside by the conversion of their lives to Christ. There are also those who are on the inside who are not real sheep, who will abandon Christ before the end, Augustine says. No one should presume, as the pagans do, that they will have eternal life if they do not enter the sheepfold through the gate (see *Homilies* 45.2, 12).

If Christ is the gate, there is no gatekeeper greater than the gate. The hireling is the one who seeks his own advantage, not Christ's. He does not dare to rebuke a sinner, for fear of losing his temporal reward (see *Homilies* 46.2, 8).

MEDITATIO

High on the mountain of faith, the air is thin, and our words falter. Concepts break apart like distant peaks swallowed by clouds. Yet there, at the summit, stands Christ—both the Gate and the Gatekeeper, the Shepherd and the Way. *"I am the door: by Me, if any man enter in, he shall be saved."*

He is the source and destiny of our salvation. He is the Alpha and Omega of our faith. To contemplate Christ is to see the whole at once, as we see the whole landscape from a mountaintop.

But the path to the summit is not passive. No one drifts upward or stumbles into eternity by chance. Christ's voice calls, but we must rise, step by step, through the hard work of conversion. His grace awakens our hearts, attuning us to His voice—gentle yet commanding.

Thieves and hirelings may try to deceive or scatter us. False guides flee at the first sign of danger, leaving us exposed on the edge of spiritual cliffs. But *"the Good Shepherd giveth His life for His sheep."* His voice cuts through every storm, steady and sure.

We must stay alert by keeping the voice of Christ in our minds and hearts. It is as easy to tumble out of the sheepfold as it is to fall down a mountainside or let the open Bible fall from our lap.

ORATIO

1. Christ calls Himself the gate and the gatekeeper; He folds two concepts together to say Who He is. Has God given me any insight I cannot put into words? Let me thank God for such a contemplative gift.

2. Each of us has a share with Christ in guarding the flock, as clergy, parents, and friends. Augustine points out specifically our role in rebuking the sinner. Do I do this? What else can I do to encourage my fellow sheep to enter the Gate?

3. Any who assert that they do not need to go through the gatekeeper that is Christ, by converting their lives and joining the Church in prayer and sacrifice, have actually made themselves a gate, the arbiter of their own salvation. Is there any important aspect of Church life or her sacraments I refuse to participate in?

CONTEMPLATIO

LECTIO: JOHN 10:22–42

Subject: Possessing Christ in Faith, Hope, and Love

22 And it was the feast of the dedication at Jerusalem: **and it was
winter.** 23 And Jesus walked in the temple, in Solomon's porch.
24 The Jews therefore came round about him, and said to him:
How long dost thou hold our souls in suspense? If thou be the
Christ, tell us plainly. 25 Jesus answered them: I speak to you, and
you believe not: the works that I do in the name of my Father, they
give testimony of me.

26 But you do not believe, because you are not of my sheep.
27 My sheep hear my voice: and I know them, and they follow
me. 28 And I give them life everlasting; and they shall not perish
for ever, and no man shall pluck them out of my hand. 29 That
which my Father hath given me, is greater than all: and no one
can snatch them out of the hand of my Father. 30 **I and the Father
are one.**

31 **The Jews then took up stones to stone him.** 32 Jesus
answered them: Many good works I have shewed you from my
Father; for which of those works do you stone me? 33 **The Jews
answered him: For a good work we stone thee not, but for blasphemy; and because that thou, being a man, makest thyself
God.** 34 **Jesus answered them: Is it not written in your law: *I
said you are gods?*** 35 **If he called them gods, to whom the word
of God was spoken, and the scripture cannot be broken;**

36 **Do you say of him whom the Father hath sanctified and
sent into the world: Thou blasphemest, because I said, I am the
Son of God?** 37 If I do not the works of my Father, believe me not.
38 But if I do, though you will not believe me, believe the works:
that you may know and believe that the Father is in me, and I in
the Father. 39 They sought therefore to take him; and he escaped
out of their hands. 40 And he went again beyond the Jordan, into
that place where John was baptizing first; and there he abode.

41 And many resorted to him, and they said: John indeed did
no sign. 42 But all things whatsoever John said of this man, were
true. And many believed in him.

Reading with St. Augustine

John the Evangelist notes that it is winter when Jesus continues this discourse on the Good Shepherd. Augustine interprets the winter scene as revealing the hearts of Jesus's listeners: "They were cold, for they were loath to approach that divine fire. . . . The soul isn't moved on feet but on feelings. They were frozen in terms of living charity and on fire with a craving to harm" (*Homilies* 48.3).

The image of Christ as warming fire continues: "If those who are warmed in some way by the fire of salvation are made gods, isn't the one warming them God?" In other words, Augustine says, those listening to Christ ought to recognize what they are responding to. They hear His claim to be one with the Father as blasphemy, and Jesus tells them they should, instead, recognize how close they are to the Father themselves (*Homilies* 48.9).

Those speaking with Christ want to seize Him, but not in the right way: "You seized him [with faith] in order to possess him; they wanted to seize him [by raging and killing] so as not to possess him. . . . To seize the Word with the mind is the right way to seize Christ" (*Homilies* 48.11).

MEDITATIO

The wind chilled the temple courts as Jesus walked through Solomon's porch. It was winter—not just in season, but in the hearts of His listeners. Their faith lay frozen, stiffened by doubt. *"How long dost Thou hold our souls in suspense? If Thou be the Christ, tell us plainly."* Their words were sharp, demanding certainty without belief.

Jesus answered with truth that burned like fire: *"I speak to you, and you believe not.* St. Augustine reflects that faith, hope, and love are divine flames, kindled only by grace. Faith sees with God's eyes, beyond sense and imagination. Hope reaches into eternity, touching life beyond time. Love desires the good of the other, expecting nothing in return.

"You are gods," Jesus declared, quoting Psalm 81:6. He did not mean power or status but participation in God's life through grace. To possess Christ is not to grasp at Him but to be united with Him—faith holding fast, hope looking forward, love opening our hands.

"I and the Father are one." His words angered the Jews. Stones rose in angry hands, but Jesus stood unshaken. The Shepherd called still, His voice steady in the winter winds, offering life beyond the storm. Only hearts willing to be warmed by love would follow.

ORATIO

1. Anything for which Jesus rebukes and instructs the listeners of His day applies to us. The winter of lovelessness may cover our own hearts in ice. Is there some place in which my own heart is frozen toward God or my neighbor?

2. How do I imagine heaven or life as a Christian on earth? Do I look forward to sensual pleasures or to a share in the godlike exercise of faith, hope, and love over the created world?

3. Do I seize Christ privately, or does my prayer and worship allow me to possess Him with my whole outward being?

CONTEMPLATIO

LECTIO: JOHN 11:1–16

Subject: Freedom in Due Course

1 **Now there was a certain man sick, named Lazarus, of Bethania, of the town of Mary and of Martha her sister.** 2 (And Mary was she that anointed the Lord with ointment, and wiped his feet with her hair: whose brother Lazarus was sick.) 3 **His sisters therefore sent to him, saying: Lord, behold, he whom thou lovest is sick.** 4 And Jesus hearing it, said to them: This sickness is not unto death, but for the glory of God: that the Son of God may be glorified by it. 5 Now Jesus loved Martha, and her sister Mary, and Lazarus.

6 When he had heard therefore that he was sick, he still remained in the same place two days. 7 Then after that, he said to his disciples: Let us go into Judea again. 8 The disciples say to him: Rabbi, the Jews but now sought to stone thee: and goest thou thither again? 9 Jesus answered: Are there not twelve hours of the day? If a man walk in the day, he stumbleth not, because he seeth the light of this world: 10 But if he walk in the night, he stumbleth, because the light is not in him.

11 These things he said; and after that he said to them: Lazarus our friend sleepeth; but I go that I may awake him out of sleep. 12 His disciples therefore said: Lord, if he sleep, he shall do well. 13 But Jesus spoke of his death; and they thought that he spoke of the repose of sleep. 14 Then therefore Jesus said to them plainly: Lazarus is dead. 15 And I am glad, for your sakes, that I was not there, that you may believe: but let us go to him.

16 Thomas therefore, who is called Didymus, said to his fellow disciples: Let us also go, that we may die with him.

Reading with St. Augustine

Augustine regularly makes the point that creation is a greater miracle than any deed God performs within it. God raises some from the dead now, though, so that all might believe in His power to raise all from the dead on the last day and to be prepared for the Resurrection unto life, the fulfillment of creation (see *Homilies* 49.1).

In the gospels, Jesus raises three different persons from the dead: the daughter of a synagogue ruler, who lies at home (see Mark 5:35–42); the young son of a widow, who is being carried through the gates of a city (see Luke 7:11–15); Lazarus, who has been buried for four days (see John 11:1–44). These three represent different stages of sin, from which our Lord raises us: consenting to a bad thought without committing an outward sin (the little girl in her home); committing a sinful outward deed (the young man being carried out); forming a habit of deadly sin (Lazarus) (see *Homilies* 49.3).

Even though Lazarus, for Augustine, represents habitual, deadly sin, Jesus loves him habitually. Martha and Mary appeal to that love: "He whom thou lovest is sick." Augustine says, "If God didn't love sinners, he wouldn't have come down from heaven to earth" (*Homilies* 49.5).

MEDITATIO

The news of Lazarus's illness reached Jesus, but He did not rush to Bethany. *"This sickness is not unto death, but for the glory of God."* His words puzzled the disciples. Days passed, and Lazarus died. *"Let us go to him,"* Jesus said at last.

St. Augustine sees Lazarus's death as a symbol of the soul trapped in habitual sin. Like a body sealed in a tomb, sin isolates, decays, and darkens the soul. Yet Jesus, the Resurrection and the Life, approaches even those long dead in sin—especially them.

Martha met Him with anxious faith, her heart divided between grief and belief. *"Lord, if Thou hadst been here, my brother had not died."* Jesus drew her closer to trust in His power—not just over life, but over death itself. Mary, marked by past sins yet filled with love, fell weeping at His feet. She trusted not in herself, but in the mercy of the One who called sinners His friends.

Jesus's love did not shrink from the stench of death or sin. He commanded the stone rolled away—not because He needed access, but to reveal His power to restore what seemed lost forever. *"Lazarus, come forth!"* His voice pierced the darkness. Just as He called Lazarus from the tomb, He calls each of us from the grave of sin. No soul is too far gone. In His mercy, Christ stands at the entrance of every heart, ready to lift the heavy stone, breathing life where death once reigned.

ORATIO

1. Thinking about our bad habits can often bring us down in spirit. Let me meditate on the close friendship Jesus has made with three people—Martha, Mary, and Lazarus—who represent habitual sin for us.

2. Augustine notes that Martha and Mary do not command Jesus to come and heal Lazarus. They only appeal to His habitual love for His friend. Let me meditate on God's constant love for me, no matter what I've done.

3. Saint Augustine, himself, suffers for many years a habit of bad behavior—ambition, sexual sins, and abandoning his concubine and son. Our Lord finally reaches him at the right moment and through the right people. If I am suffering a vicious habit, let me pray for the patience to wait for God's help at the right time.

CONTEMPLATIO

LECTIO: JOHN 11:17–37

Subject: Rising from Sin with Christ

17 **Jesus therefore came, and found that he had been four days already in the grave.** 18 (Now Bethania was near Jerusalem, about fifteen furlongs off.) 19 And many of the Jews were come to Martha and Mary, to comfort them concerning their brother. 20 Martha therefore, as soon as she heard that Jesus was come, went to meet him: but Mary sat at home.

21 Martha therefore said to Jesus: Lord, if thou hadst been here, my brother had not died. 22 But now also I know that whatsoever thou wilt ask of God, God will give it thee. 23 Jesus saith to her: Thy brother shall rise again. 24 Martha saith to him: I know that he shall rise again, in the resurrection at the last day. 25 Jesus said to her: I am the resurrection and the life: he that believeth in me, although he be dead, shall live:

26 And every one that liveth, and believeth in me, shall not die for ever. Believest thou this? 27 She saith to him: Yea, Lord, I have believed that thou art Christ the Son of the living God, who art come into this world. 28 And when she had said these things, she went, and called her sister Mary secretly, saying: The master is come, and calleth for thee. 29 She, as soon as she heard this, riseth quickly, and cometh to him. 30 For Jesus was not yet come into the town: but he was still in that place where Martha had met him.

31 The Jews therefore, who were with her in the house, and comforted her, when they saw Mary that she rose up speedily and went out, followed her, saying: She goeth to the grave to weep there. 32 When Mary therefore was come where Jesus was, seeing him, she fell down at his feet, and saith to him: Lord, if thou hadst been here, my brother had not died. 33 **Jesus, therefore, when he saw her weeping, and the Jews that were come with her, weeping, groaned in the spirit, and troubled himself,** 34 And said: Where have you laid him? They say to him: Lord, come and see. 35 And Jesus wept.

36 The Jews therefore said: Behold how he loved him. 37 But some of them said: Could not he that opened the eyes of the man born blind, have caused that this man should not die?

Reading with St. Augustine

Meditating on the meaning of the four days that Lazarus is in the tomb, Augustine shows us four days of sin in the life of humanity: on the first day, we are born into a state of sin; then, we arrive at the age of reason, when we should understand we should do unto others as we want them to do unto us, and we transgress this natural law; then, we receive the law of Moses and break those commandments; finally, we receive the Gospel and treat it with contempt (see *Homilies* 49.12).

Augustine takes us inside the tomb to consider in what conditions souls are held until the general Resurrection. Some are held under light guard and others under more serious guard, according to their personal history, and are given recompense at the Resurrection according to that personal history. We are each judged individually after death, but at the Resurrection, "The joy of good [souls] will be amplified, the torments of the bad [souls] will be more oppressive, since they will be tormented with their body" (*Homilies* 49.9–10).

Augustine tells us that while we respond passively to our moods and emotions, Jesus wills all that He experiences. If John writes that Jesus "groaned in the spirit, and troubled himself," it is to teach us to weep over sin and death (see *Homilies* 49.18–19).

MEDITATIO

The air in Bethany was thick with mourning as Martha hurried to meet Jesus. Her face was etched with grief, but her words clung to hope: *"Lord, if Thou hadst been here, my brother had not died."* Her faith strained against the finality of death, reaching for something beyond her understanding.

"I am the resurrection and the life," Jesus declared, His voice steady and sure. *"He that believeth in Me, although he be dead, shall live."* He was not speaking of a distant hope but a present reality—the very source of life standing before her. Martha believed, though the weight of her sorrow remained.

On Holy Saturday, tradition holds that Jesus harrows hell and brings to salvation the holy men and women who have died before Christ comes. They were subject to original sin, they sinned against reason and expressed commandments (John the Evangelist reminds us we all sin; see 1 Jn. 1:8), and they were ignorant of the Gospel. Augustine interprets Lazarus's four days in the tomb as these four stages of sin. Tradition holds that even though Christ preached the Gospel to all in the tomb, only the righteous gained heaven.

Martha and Mary are sad because their brother is dead. Jesus chooses to groan and weep to teach us all to hate sin and loathe death. We who have heard the Gospel should never presume on God's forgiveness but seek it out and choose to loathe sin now. We are joined to Christ, the resurrection and the life, and should weep for all who are not.

ORATIO

1. Just as there are some who act against reason with selfish behavior, there are some who hold Gospel values in contempt. Let me groan and weep with Jesus for their salvation and mine.

2. Let me choose to hate my own sins and the death they bring.

3. Jesus is the resurrection and the life. Let me meditate on enjoying heaven not simply as a reward for my good behavior, but as a share in God's own life, power, joy, and majesty.

CONTEMPLATIO

LECTIO: JOHN 11:38–54

Subject: Bound in Pride

[38] **Jesus therefore again groaning in himself, cometh** to the sepulchre. Now it was a cave; **and a stone was laid over it.** [39] **Jesus saith: Take away the stone.** Martha, the sister of him that was dead, saith to him: Lord, by this time he stinketh, for he is now of four days. [40] Jesus saith to her: Did not I say to thee, that if thou believe, thou shalt see the glory of God?

[41] **They took therefore the stone away.** And Jesus lifting up his eyes said: Father, I give thee thanks that thou hast heard me. [42] And I knew that thou hearest me always; but because of the people who stand about have I said it, that they may believe that thou hast sent me. [43] When he had said these things, he cried with a loud voice: Lazarus, come forth. [44] **And presently he that had been dead came forth, bound feet and hands with winding bands; and his face was bound about with a napkin. Jesus said to them: Loose him, and let him go.** [45] Many therefore of the Jews, who were come to Mary and Martha, and had seen the things that Jesus did, believed in him.

[46] But some of them went to the Pharisees, and told them the things that Jesus had done. [47] The chief priests therefore, and the Pharisees, gathered a council, and said: What do we, for this man doth many miracles? [48] If we let him alone so, all will believe in him; and the Romans will come, and take away our place and nation. [49] But one of them, named Caiphas, being the high priest that year, said to them: You know nothing. [50] Neither do you consider that it is expedient for you that one man should die for the people, and that the whole nation perish not.

[51] And this he spoke not of himself: but being the high priest of that year, he prophesied that Jesus should die for the nation. [52] And not only for the nation, but to gather together in one the children of God, that were dispersed. [53] From that day therefore they devised to put him to death. [54] Wherefore Jesus walked no more openly among the Jews; but he went into a country near the desert, unto a city that is called Ephrem, and there he abode with his disciples.

Reading with St. Augustine

Augustine returns to the purpose of Christ's groaning: "What, then, does it mean that Christ troubles himself if not to signify to you that you should be troubled when you are weighed down and crushed by such a great weight of sin?" The groaning is the voice of faith: "If faith itself is within, Christ is there groaning" (*Homilies* 49.19).

The stone stands in for the weight of our habitual sins and also of the law. The command by Jesus to remove the stone means, "Preach grace" (*Homilies* 49.22).

Lazarus comes out of the tomb still bound. Jesus's command to loosen the bonds means to forgive him his sins (see *Homilies* 49.24).

MEDITATIO

The raising of Lazarus from the dead is the last sign that Jesus performs openly and the one that finally leads to His death. It is an illustration of what Jesus does for us by His death, forgiving our sins and freeing us from the bonds of habitual sin. The law on its own cannot accomplish this.

St. Augustine shows that Jesus allowed Lazarus to remain in the tomb, wrapped in death's stench, so that no one could deny the power of His grace (*Homilies* 49.9). The rot of Lazarus's body mirrors the corruption of the soul trapped in habitual sin—foul, hopeless, bound in spiritual death.

"Lazarus, come forth!" Jesus cried, His voice breaking through stone and darkness. Lazarus stumbled into the light, still wrapped in burial cloths. *"Loose him, and let him go."* It was not enough to be raised—he had to be set free.

The law alone, like the heavy stone, cannot break the bonds of sin. The law shows what is wrong but cannot restore the sinner's soul. Augustine reminds us that even Paul, the great apostle, wrestled with sin's grip, calling it *"a thorn of Satan"* that kept him humble (2 Cor. 12:7).

Jesus, the Resurrection and the Life, calls each of us from spiritual death. He lets us feel the weight of sin, the heavy stone of guilt, not to crush us, but to awaken our need for His mercy. His grace alone can break every chain, raising us into the light of new life. In His love, we are no longer bound—we are free.

ORATIO

1. Groaning and weeping over sins are an act of faith in God, Who has made us for charity and virtue. Let me find a bad situation that moves me—war, injustice, greed, famine, disaster, the promotion of sin, for example—and pray about it with the groaning of Christ within me.

2. The authorities who hate Jesus represent a form of legalism that cannot save Lazarus. Have I bound myself excessively to the observation of the law in any aspect of my life? Is there some religious observance that has become a point of spiritual pride for me? What does grace ask of me instead?

CONTEMPLATIO

LECTIO: JOHN 11:5–56; 12:1–11

Subject: Living Inner Faith Outwardly

[55] And the pasch of the Jews was at hand; and many from the country went up to Jerusalem, before the pasch to purify themselves.

[56] They sought therefore for Jesus; and they discoursed one with another, standing in the temple: What think you that he is not come to the festival day? And the chief priests and Pharisees had given a commandment, that if any man knew where he was, he should tell, that they might apprehend him.

Chapter 12

[1] Jesus therefore, six days before the pasch, came to Bethania,
where Lazarus had been dead, whom Jesus raised to life. [2] And
they made him a supper there: and Martha served: but Lazarus
was one of them that were at table with him. [3] **Mary therefore
took a pound of ointment of right spikenard, of great price,
and anointed the feet of Jesus, and wiped his feet with her
hair; and the house was filled with the odour of the ointment.**
[4] **Then one of his disciples, Judas Iscariot, he that was about to
betray him, said:** [5] **Why was not this ointment sold for three
hundred pence, and given to the poor?**

[6] **Now he said this, not because he cared for the poor; but
because he was a thief, and having the purse, carried the things
that were put therein.** [7] Jesus therefore said: Let her alone, that
she may keep it against the day of my burial. [8] For the poor you
have always with you; but me you have not always. [9] A great multitude therefore of the Jews knew that he was there; and they came,
not for Jesus' sake only, but that they might see Lazarus, whom he
had raised from the dead. [10] But the chief priests thought to kill
Lazarus also:

[11] Because many of the Jews, by reason of him, went away, and believed in Jesus.

Reading with St. Augustine

Augustine finds in this passage an opportunity to reflect on the outward expression of our inner faith. It is the feast of Passover, when people mark their doorposts with the blood of a lamb. If we mark ourselves with Christ outwardly, we must all the more welcome Him in our heart (see *Homilies* 50.2).

Augustine sees in Mary's perfume justice, and in the spikenard, faith. Likewise, we should express our inward faith with Mary: "Anoint the feet of Jesus; follow in the Lord's footsteps by living a good life. Dry his feet with your hair; if you have a surplus, give to the poor, and you have dried the Lord's feet, for hair seems to be superfluous to the body." We should fill the earth with the fragrance of a good reputation as Christians (*Homilies* 50.6–7).

Judas follows Jesus with his body but not with his heart. He does not perish only when he sells Jesus for thirty pieces of silver; he is already a thief and one who is envious of another person doing good (see *Homilies* 50.8–10).

MEDITATIO

The house in Bethany was filled with the fragrance of precious ointment. Mary of Bethany knelt at Jesus's feet, pouring out a jar of costly spikenard, her hands trembling with devotion. With every drop, she anointed Him—not just as a king, but for His coming Passion. Her silent act spoke a love deeper than words.

St. Augustine sees in Mary the perfect union of inward faith and outward worship. Her act was both spiritual and physical, a complete offering of heart and hands. She gave extravagantly, not measuring the cost, because love, real love, cannot be weighed or counted.

But Judas did measure. *"Why was this ointment not sold for three hundred pence and given to the poor?"* he objected, his voice laced with hidden greed. His heart was tipped toward self-interest, masking envy with false concern for justice. He was prioritizing outward actions over inner belief.

Jesus's answer was piercing: *"The poor you have always with you, but Me you have not always."* He saw beyond Judas's pretense and honored Mary's unreserved gift. Her outward action mirrored an inward faith that recognized Jesus's coming sacrifice.

Augustine warns that we, too, can fall into Judas's trap—judging others' offerings, dismissing acts of love as wasteful. True devotion flows from a heart emptied of pride and filled with faith. Like Mary, we are called to anoint Christ—not with measured gestures, but with lives poured out in love, body and soul.

ORATIO

1. Are there ways, even extravagant ways, I can be demonstrating my inward faith?

2. Do I do make any outward displays of faith and charity to conceal my inner envy or greed?

3. Have I detracted from the good reputation of another Christian in the world?

CONTEMPLATIO

LECTIO: JOHN 12:12–19

Subject: The Condescension of the King

12 And on the next day, a great multitude that was come to the festival day, when they had heard that Jesus was coming to Jerusalem,
13 **Took branches of palm trees, and went forth to meet him,
and cried: Hosanna, blessed is he that cometh in the name of
the Lord, the king of Israel.** 14 **And Jesus found a young ass,
and sat upon it, as it is written:** 15 ***Fear not, daughter of Sion:
behold, thy king cometh, sitting on an ass's colt.***

16 These things his disciples did not know at the first; but
when Jesus was glorified, then they remembered that these things
were written of him, and that they had done these things to him.
17 The multitude therefore gave testimony, which was with him,
when he called Lazarus out of the grave, and raised him from the
dead. 18 For which reason also the people came to meet him, because they heard that he had done this miracle. 19 The Pharisees
therefore said among themselves: Do you see that we prevail nothing? behold, the whole world is gone after him.

Reading with St. Augustine

Augustine inverts our expectations of what Christ is doing with His triumphal entry into Jerusalem. That the Son of God "willed to be king of Israel was a matter of condescension, not advancement, a measure of his compassion, not an augmentation of his power. For the one who was called king of the Jews on earth is the Lord of the angels in heaven" (*Homilies* 51.4).

The foal upon which Jesus rides, upon which the other evangelists tell us no one had sat (see Mark 11:2), Augustine takes as the gentiles, who had not received the law of the Lord, and the donkey from which the foal issues is the nation of Israel, which earlier recognizes the Lord's crib (see Is. 1:3; Luke 2:16) (see *Homilies* 51.5).

MEDITATIO

The air buzzed with excitement as Jesus rode into Jerusalem on a young donkey, fulfilling ancient prophecy: *"Fear not, daughter of Sion: behold, thy King cometh, sitting upon an ass's colt."* Crowds surged forward, waving palm branches and shouting, *"Hosanna! Blessed is He that cometh in the name of the Lord!"* They celebrated a king—but saw only through earthly eyes.

St. Augustine warns that the people followed Jesus for the wrong reason.. They marveled at the raising of Lazarus but missed the greater truth: Jesus had come not to claim power, but to surrender it. They saw a political liberator, not the Suffering Servant.

The palms they waved in triumph would soon fall to the ground, trampled underfoot as their *"Hosannas"* turned to *"Crucify Him!"* They misunderstood kingship itself. When one of their own rose to power, it became a source of pride. But when the Creator donned a mock royal cloak, it meant suffering, mockery, and death.

The facts of Jesus's entry are undeniable—but how we see them makes all the difference. Augustine reminds us that singing *"Hosanna"* at Holy Mass means far more than the crowd's fleeting cries. We receive Christ not as a passing miracle-worker, but as the Lamb of God who comes to take away our sins. To welcome Him in faith is to crown Him—not with earthly laurels, but with hearts transformed by grace. We receive Jesus with faith at Holy Mass, so long as we do not turn from Him in our sin like the old crowd does.

ORATIO

1. John the Evangelist has led me, so far, on a different path from the other gospels. Have I felt disoriented or lost? Has Augustine helped me keep my bearings? Am I glad for a moment of contact with the other gospels?

2. Do I enjoy a position of leadership in this world, and if so, from whose perspective do I enjoy it—that of the adulation of the crowd, or that of Jesus, Who knows His leadership is a position of humility and self-sacrifice? With Jesus, can I let the crowd forget or insult me for the sake of doing what is right and charitable?

3. All of the events of Jesus's earthly life draw upon the types and figures of the Old Testament, and they inform and give life to what we

do in the Church today. Every Eucharist is a reliving of Jesus's passion, death, and resurrection. Let me meditate on the importance of what my church offers me every day.

CONTEMPLATIO

LECTIO: JOHN 12:20–36

Subject: Preparing for the Passion

20 Now there were certain Gentiles among them, who came up to
adore on the festival day. 21 These therefore came to Philip, who
was of Bethsaida of Galilee, and desired him, saying: Sir, we would
see Jesus. 22 Philip cometh, and telleth Andrew. Again Andrew and
Philip told Jesus. 23 But Jesus answered them, saying: The hour is
come, that the Son of man should be glorified. 24 Amen, amen I
say to you, unless the grain of wheat falling into the ground die,
25 Itself remaineth alone. But if it die, it bringeth forth much fruit.
He that loveth his life shall lose it; and he that hateth his life in this
world, keepeth it unto life eternal.

26 **If any man minister to me, let him follow me; and where**
I am, there also shall my minister be. If any man minister to
me, him will my Father honour. 27 **Now is my soul troubled.**
And what shall I say? Father, save me from this hour. But for this
cause I came unto this hour. 28 Father, glorify thy name. **A voice**
therefore came from heaven: I have both glorified it, and will
glorify it again. 29 The multitude therefore that stood and heard,
said that it thundered. Others said: An angel spoke to him. 30 Jesus
answered, and said: This voice came not because of me, but for
your sakes.

31 **Now is the judgment of the world: now shall the prince**
of this world be cast out. 32 And I, if I be lifted up from the earth,
will draw all things to myself. 33 (Now this he said, signifying what
death he should die.) 34 The multitude answered him: We have
heard out of the law, that Christ abideth for ever; and how sayest
thou: The Son of man must be lifted up? Who is this Son of man?
35 Jesus therefore said to them: Yet a little while, the light is among
you. Walk whilst you have the light, that the darkness overtake
you not. And he that walketh in darkness, knoweth not whither
he goeth.

36 Whilst you have the light, believe in the light, that you may
be the children of light. These things Jesus spoke; and he went
away, and hid himself from them.

Reading with St. Augustine

Augustine reminds us that external forms of service are not enough; we must remove all self-serving intentions from charity's work. Martha does herself no good acting as a busybody. Judas holds the purse and, despite speaking up for the poor, is greedy for gain. On the other hand, Augustine says, no matter our state in life, we can serve as a minister of Christ, and in fact, every parent who admonishes, teaches, encourages, and shows kindness to those in his care acts as a bishop for them (see *Homilies* 51.12–13).

Just as Jesus troubles His soul for our sake and not His own, so too when God the Father speaks, He does so for those gathered around Jesus. Augustine says that the first glory God gives Jesus is at His epiphanies in the Flesh—at the visit of the magi, at His baptism, and at His transfiguration—while the second is at His return in glory, when "he will be exalted as God above the heavens" (*Homilies* 52.4–5).

The judgment of the world is that Jesus has cast out the devil from it. Augustine identifies the world not as the planet itself, which God rules, but the people who live in the world (just as we identify a house with the people who live inside it). The devil is cast out of those who believe in Jesus; we should not presume on our own strength, then, or we may summon the devil back in (see *Homilies* 52.7–10).

MEDITATIO

The air in Jerusalem buzzed with anticipation as Greeks approached Philip, asking, *"Sir, we would see Jesus."* Their request signaled that Christ's mission was reaching beyond Israel, drawing the world toward Him. In response, Jesus spoke of His coming hour—not of triumph as the world imagined, but of sacrifice: *"Unless the grain of wheat falling into the ground die, itself remaineth alone."*

St. Augustine shows that Jesus's death would not be the end but the beginning of His full glorification. At His baptism, the Father's voice declared Him *"My beloved Son."* Though the Transfiguration is absent from John's Gospel, the Father's silent assurance remains. Now, at the threshold of the Cross, the Father speaks again through His Son's resolve.

"Father, glorify Thy name." The heavens thundered: *"I have glorified it, and will glorify it again."* The crowd, confused, heard only noise—but Jesus understood. The Father's voice was not for Him but for them—and for us.

We, too, live in the time between His earthly mission and His promised return. Augustine reminds us that as priests of our own households, we must guide others toward the light through word, deed, and sacrifice. Darkness still resists, but *"the prince of this world is cast out."*

"Walk while you have the light," Jesus urged. His path leads through suffering but ends in eternal glory. As His disciples, we follow—not in fear, but in hope, bearing His light for all to see.

ORATIO

1. When Philip brings some gentiles to Jesus, the Blessed Trinity takes the occasion to encourage everyone gathered for the age to come after Jesus's passion, death, and resurrection. In what way do I minister to Christ in this age?

2. Let me imagine I am one of the Greeks Philip has brought to Christ. Perhaps I know a little about Jesus already. Now I hear the voice of God speaking about Him. How does my heart move?

3. After the Father speaks, Jesus says that the prince of this world is cast out. When I look around my world, what difference has this judgment made—or can it make, by my participation?

CONTEMPLATIO

LECTIO: JOHN 12:37–50

Subject: Faith and Free Will

37 And whereas he had done so many miracles before them, they
believed not in him: 38 **That the saying of Isaias the prophet**
might be fulfilled, which he said: ***Lord, who hath believed our***
hearing? and to whom hath the arm of the Lord been revealed?
39 **Therefore they could not believe, because Isaias said again:**

40 ***He hath blinded their eyes, and hardened their heart,***
that they should not see with their eyes, nor understand with
their heart, and be converted, and I should heal them. 41 These
things said Isaias, when he saw his glory, and spoke of him. 42 However, many of the chief men also believed in him; but because of
the Pharisees they did not confess him, that they might not be cast
out of the synagogue. 43 For they loved the glory of men more than
the glory of God. **44 But Jesus cried, and said: He that believeth**
in me, doth not believe in me, but in him that sent me. 45 **And**
he that seeth me, seeth him that sent me.

46 **I am come a light into the world; that whosoever belie-**
veth in me, may not remain in darkness. 47 **And if any man hear**
my words, and keep them not, I do not judge him: for I came
not to judge the world, but to save the world. 48 **He that de-**
spiseth me, and receiveth not my words, hath one that judgeth
him; the word that I have spoken, the same shall judge him in
the last day. 49 For I have not spoken of myself; but the Father
who sent me, he gave me commandment what I should say, and
what I should speak. 50 And I know that his commandment is life
everlasting. The things therefore that I speak, even as the Father
said unto me, so do I speak.

Reading with St. Augustine

Augustine confronts something that continues to perplex us today, God's foreknowledge and our free will. The prophet Isaiah predicts those who will not believe in Christ. Augustine says that just because God foretells something does not mean He causes it. The prideful denial of our need for divine assistance is what hardens our heart against faith (see *Homilies* 53.4, 10).

To believe in Christ is to believe in the Father, because what we believe about Christ is not limited to His humanity but also encompasses His divinity. We see the Father in the same light that illuminates Christ (see *Homilies* 52.4; 54.2).

Augustine asks why Christ does not judge the world now and discovers two periods: this period of mercy and a later time of judgment (see *Homilies* 54.5).

MEDITATIO

The temple shadows lengthened as Jesus spoke, His voice steady but urgent. He knew the hearts before Him—some hardened by pride, others softened by hope. *"I am come a light into the world,"* He declared, *"that whosoever believeth in Me may not remain in darkness."* The light burned bright, but many turned away, fearing the opinion of others more than the call of truth.

This moment reveals both mercy and warning. Jesus does not yet come as judge, though judgment is near. He comes as Savior, holding back condemnation so the Church can spread His Gospel, offering light to all who will receive it.

"For I came not to judge the world, but to save the world." His mission is life, not destruction. He speaks the commandment given by the Father—the commandment that *"is life everlasting."* Augustine sees Jesus Himself as that commandment, the living Word through whom life flows.

We, too, are called to bear this light in the age of the Church. Frustration may creep in when our words seem unheard, when darkness appears unyielding. But Jesus troubles Himself more for our salvation than we ever could. He has entrusted His life-giving Word to us—not to force belief, but to offer new life in grace.

The light shines still. The Father speaks through the Son, and His command remains: *"Walk while you have the light . . . believe in the light, that you may be children of light."* He puts off His judgment so the Church can perform the work of mercy in proclaiming the Gospel.

ORATIO

1. In what ways have I given life to this world?

2. Have I encountered anyone who would not listen to my speaking the Gospel? What words or actions have been the most effective?

3. In what ways have I exercised Christ's mercy in this age of the Church?

CONTEMPLATIO

LECTIO: JOHN 13:1–20

Subject: Purifying Our Emotions with Humility

1 Before the festival day of the pasch, Jesus knowing that his hour was come, that he should pass out of this world to the Father: having loved his own who were in the world, he loved them unto the end. 2 And when supper was done, **(the devil having now put into the heart of Judas Iscariot, the son of Simon, to betray him,)** 3 Knowing that the Father had given him all things into his hands, and that he came from God, and goeth to God; 4 **He riseth from supper, and layeth aside his garments, and having taken a towel, girded himself.** 5 **After that, he putteth water into a basin, and began to wash the feet of the disciples, and to wipe them with the towel wherewith he was girded.**

6 He cometh therefore to Simon Peter. And Peter saith to him: Lord, dost thou wash my feet? 7 Jesus answered, and said to him: What I do thou knowest not now; but thou shalt know hereafter. 8 Peter saith to him: Thou shalt never wash my feet. Jesus answered him: If I wash thee not, thou shalt have no part with me. 9 Simon Peter saith to him: Lord, not only my feet, but also my hands and my head. 10 **Jesus saith to him: He that is washed, needeth not but to wash his feet, but is clean wholly. And you are clean, but not all.**

11 For he knew who he was that would betray him; therefore he said: You are not all clean. 12 Then after he had washed their feet, and taken his garments, being set down again, he said to them: Know you what I have done to you? 13 You call me Master, and Lord; and you say well, for so I am. 14 **If then I being your Lord and Master, have washed your feet; you also ought to wash one another's feet.** 15 For I have given you an example, that as I have done to you, so you do also.

16 Amen, amen I say to you: The servant is not greater than his lord; neither is the apostle greater than he that sent him. 17 If you know these things, you shall be blessed if you do them. 18 **I speak not of you all: I know whom I have chosen. But that the scripture may be fulfilled:** ***He that eateth bread with me, shall lift up his heel against me.*** 19 At present I tell you, before it come to pass: that when it shall come to pass, you may believe that I am he. 20 Amen, amen I say to you, he that receiveth whomsoever I

send, receiveth me; and he that receiveth me, receiveth him that sent me.

Reading with St. Augustine

At the beginning and end of this passage, John confronts us with Judas's betrayal and the devil's grip on him. Augustine tells us not to wonder at how the spiritual suggestions of the devil are mixed up with our own thoughts in our mind, because good suggestions come that way, too. What matters is to which thoughts our mind consents (see *Homilies* 55.4).

Augustine tells us not to be surprised that Jesus has laid aside His garments, girded Himself with a towel, and washed His disciples' feet. This is the same Son of God Who, though in the form of God, empties Himself and takes the form of a slave, is stripped of His garments and crucified, wrapped in linen and buried (see Phil. 2:5–11) (see *Homilies* 55.7).

For Augustine, the feet signify our emotions. We are washed spiritually in Baptism, but the emotions are where our spirit meets the road of this world. For the apostles, this means humility in preaching, where boastfulness may enter. Our best protection against pride is to bend over at a brother's feet (see *Homilies* 56.4; 57.2).

MEDITATIO

Jesus has prepared the crowds to receive His coming passion, death, and resurrection by inviting the Father to speak for all to hear, Jews and Gentiles. Now Jesus speaks with His disciples in private. The upper room was dimly lit, its air heavy with expectation. Jesus rose from the table. The disciples watched in puzzled silence as He removed His outer garments and tied a linen towel around His waist. Then He knelt, pouring water into a basin. The Master had become a servant.

The abasement of the eternal and infinite Son of God is shown to his Apostles and will be shown to the world in the coming crucifixion. Jesus's disciples must imitate Him. St. Augustine sees in this act the mystery of the Incarnation itself. The eternal Son of God, clothed in divine majesty, stripped Himself of glory to take on our frail humanity. Now, on the eve of His Passion, He humbled Himself even further, washing the feet of men who would soon abandon Him.

Our emotions are the bridge between our bodies and souls, just as feet are the bridge between our bodies and the earth. Things of this world stir us to love, hate, fear, courage, envy, joy, and pride. Before Jesus preaches His long, last sermon to His disciples, He shows what attitude they must take before they, too, preach to others. Humility cleanses our emotions. Judas is greedy, angry, and fearful. The devil has worked his suggestions into Judas's mind because Judas does not cleanse his emotions or discern what comes from within and what from without.

Jesus's command echoed in the stillness: *"As I have done to you, so you also must do."* His humility cleanses; His love restores. Like Peter, when fear and sin overtake us, we must let His mercy wash over us, rising again to follow the path of service and grace—feet cleansed, hearts made new.

ORATIO

1. Are there emotions over which I have little control, like fear, envy, or anger? Do these lead me to sin?

2. What gesture of humility might help cleanse my emotions?

3. Do I lead, teach, or preach to others? In what ways does pride enter me, and where can I humble myself?

CONTEMPLATIO

LECTIO: JOHN 13:21–38

Subject: Seeing Past Scandal with Love

21 When Jesus had said these things, he was troubled in spirit; and he testified, and said: Amen, amen I say to you, one of you shall betray me. 22 The disciples therefore looked one upon another, doubting of whom he spoke. 23 Now there was leaning on Jesus' bosom one of his disciples, whom Jesus loved. 24 Simon Peter therefore beckoned to him, and said to him: Who is it of whom he speaketh? 25 He therefore, leaning on the breast of Jesus, saith to him: Lord, who is it?

26 Jesus answered: He it is to whom I shall reach bread dipped. And when he had dipped the bread, he gave it to Judas Iscariot, the son of Simon. 27 **And after the morsel, Satan entered into him. And Jesus said to him: That which thou dost, do quickly.** 28 **Now no man at the table knew to what purpose he said this unto him.** 29 For some thought, because Judas had the purse, that Jesus had said to him: Buy those things which we have need of for the festival day: or that he should give something to the poor. 30 He therefore having received the morsel, went out immediately. And it was night.

31 When he therefore was gone out, Jesus said: Now is the Son of man glorified, and God is glorified in him. 32 If God be glorified in him, God also will glorify him in himself; and immediately will he glorify him. 33 Little children, yet a little while I am with you. You shall seek me; and as I said to the Jews: Whither I go you cannot come; so I say to you now. 34 **A new commandment I give unto you: That you love one another, as I have loved you, that you also love one another.** 35 By this shall all men know that you are my disciples, if you have love one for another.

36 Simon Peter saith to him: Lord, whither goest thou? Jesus answered: Whither I go, thou canst not follow me now; but thou shalt follow hereafter. 37 **Peter saith to him: Why cannot I follow thee now? I will lay down my life for thee.** 38 Jesus answered him: Wilt thou lay down thy life for me? Amen, amen I say to thee, the cock shall not crow, till thou deny me thrice.

Reading with St. Augustine

Our inner disposition toward what we receive matters as much as what we receive, Augustine says regarding Judas. Jesus gives him the Eucharist, and Satan enters into him. The Eucharist is good for good people and harmful to bad people. Likewise, when Paul is given a devil to make him suffer (see 2 Cor. 12:7), it only does Paul good, because he receives it humbly and prayerfully (see *Homilies* 62.1).

In a scandal like this, Augustine says, "Spiritual persons who belong to the Lord are troubled not by perversity but by charity, for fear that, perhaps, in the separation of some of the weeds, some of the wheat may also be uprooted at the same time." In other words, it is better that the other disciples do not know why Judas has left the table until later, when their faith is secure (*Homilies* 61.1).

Peter asks to follow the Lord, but Jesus teaches him the way there by commanding the disciples to love one another. Jesus is going through death into life, and the love He teaches is such a form of death: "If that is death when the soul leaves the body, how is it not death when our love leaves the world?" (*Homilies* 65.1).

MEDITATIO

The Apostles grew tense as Jesus spoke: *"One of you shall betray Me."* His words hung heavy, cutting through the intimate gathering like a blade. The Apostles exchanged uncertain glances, fear tightening their throats. Peter, always bold, signaled to John: *"Who is it whom he speaketh?"*

Jesus answered quietly: *"He it is to whom I shall give the morsel."* He dipped the bread and handed it to Judas, whose eyes flickered with something darker than doubt. Scripture tells us, *"Satan entered into him."*

Judas's betrayal was not predestined but chosen, a tragic misuse of freedom. Even in that last moment, Jesus offered him the sacred morsel—a sign of shared fellowship. The same grace given to Peter was offered to Judas, but where Peter would fall and rise in repentance, Judas would fall and despair.

Even before the disciples can feel the wound of Judas's departure, Jesus teaches them the law by which He holds the Church together, *"A new commandment I give unto you,"* Jesus continued, *"that you love one another, as I have loved you."* This love is a form of death. Augustine calls it *"death to the world,"* the surrender that leads to true freedom. Peter will die this loving death when he repents of denying Christ and when Jesus commands him, in love, to feed His sheep.

Dying to this world perfects our freedom and therefore our faith. The witness of a perfect faith often overpowers the doubts of even the hardest hearts we encounter and serves as medicine for the wounded.

ORATIO

1. What do I ask the grace of God's sacraments to do for me?

2. Has the work of a Judas or the sin of a Peter scandalized me? What sustains my faith?

3. In what ways has God called me to love my brother or sister more perfectly, to die to this world more fully?

CONTEMPLATIO

LECTIO: JOHN 14:1–14

Subject: Preparing the Way within Us

1 Let not your heart be troubled. You believe in God: believe also in me. 2 **In my Father's house there are many mansions.** If not, I would have told you: because I go to prepare a place for you. 3 And if I shall go, and prepare a place for you, I will come again, and will take you to myself; that where I am, you also may be. 4 And whither I go you know, and the way you know. 5 **Thomas saith to him: Lord, we know not whither thou goest; and how can we know the way?**

6 **Jesus saith to him: I am the way, and the truth, and the life. No man cometh to the Father, but by me.** 7 If you had known me, you would without doubt have known my Father also: and from henceforth you shall know him, and you have seen him. 8 Philip saith to him: Lord, shew us the Father, and it is enough for us. 9 Jesus saith to him: Have I been so long a time with you; and have you not known me? Philip, he that seeth me seeth the Father also. How sayest thou, Shew us the Father? 10 Do you not believe, that I am in the Father, and the Father in me? The words that I speak to you, I speak not of myself. But the Father who abideth in me, he doth the works.

11 Believe you not that I am in the Father, and the Father in me? 12 Otherwise believe for the very works' sake. **Amen, amen I say to you, he that believeth in me, the works that I do, he also shall do; and greater than these shall he do.** 13 **Because I go to the Father: and whatsoever you shall ask the Father in my name, that will I do: that the Father may be glorified in the Son.** 14 If you shall ask me any thing in my name, that I will do.

Reading with St. Augustine

Augustine, reflecting on the many mansions of the Father's house, shows us that just as the different bodies in the sky—the sun, the moon, the stars—have different degrees of glory, so the saints are allotted different dwellings of splendor. However, "each one also possesses what he himself doesn't possess when he loves it in another." In other words, just as the moon enjoys the light of the sun, each of us will enjoy each other's heavenly light (*Homilies* 67.2).

Thomas asks what the way is that Jesus is taking, and Jesus says that He Himself is the Way, the Truth, and the Life. Augustine ponders what way Jesus could be preparing and concludes that it is us that Jesus is preparing, by faith. Jesus takes Himself from our sight in order to perfect our faith and make our hearts long for Him with greater love: "Love's longing is the preparation of the dwelling" (*Homilies* 68.3).

The saints will do greater things than Jesus does because Jesus is acting in them, and the people to whom Jesus sends the saints receive them better than they receive Jesus when He speaks to them: "See, he did greater things when he was proclaimed by believers than when he spoke to his hearers" (*Homilies* 72.1).

MEDITATIO

The upper room was quiet as Jesus spoke: *"Let not your heart be troubled."* His disciples listened, anxious and confused. He had just foretold Peter's denial and hinted at His coming departure. How could they not be troubled?

"I go to prepare a place for you." The words hung like a promise, though they scarcely understood. Thomas, ever practical, voiced what they all wondered: *"Lord, we know not whither Thou goest; and how can we know the way?"*

"I am the way, and the truth, and the life," Jesus answered. *"No man cometh to the Father but by Me."*

The way Jesus is preparing, Augustine says, is within the disciples. Jesus must leave their sight in order to open up this path. He must leave their sight so they can walk by faith, longing for the One they cannot see. Love grows stronger in absence; faith deepens when the beloved is unseen.

In heaven, we will shine according to our love and faith. Augustine likens it to the light of the sun and moon—each reflecting divine glory, without envy or pride. Every saint's brilliance will be a shared joy.

"Show us the Father," Philip pleaded. Jesus's voice softened: *"He that seeth Me seeth the Father."*

Jesus's work continues through feeble hands, His Church. The apostles, and we, become His living path—imperfect yet chosen. Though we may stumble, His light never fails. He goes ahead, preparing a place, drawing us by love into the Father's eternal home.

ORATIO

1. "Love's longing is the preparation of the dwelling," Augustine says. What does my longing for God feel like?

2. "In my Father's house there are many mansions." Do I rejoice in the gifts God has given to those around me, the light that others shine for me? Let me meditate on them.

3. Do I feel frustrated that some good I am trying to accomplish seems fruitless? Let me give this to the Lord in His patience, since His own Gospel bears fruit through others.

CONTEMPLATIO

LECTIO: JOHN 14:15–31

SUBJECT: SEEKING TRUTH IN THE SPIRIT

15 If you love me, keep my commandments.

16 And I will ask the Father, and he shall give you another Paraclete, that he may abide with you for ever. 17 The spirit of truth, whom the world cannot receive, because it seeth him not, nor knoweth him: but you shall know him; because he shall abide with you, and shall be in you. 18 I will not leave you orphans, I will come to you. 19 Yet a little while: and the world seeth me no more. But you see me: because I live, and you shall live. 20 In that day you shall know, that I am in my Father, and you in me, and I in you.

21 He that hath my commandments, and keepeth them; he it is that loveth me. And he that loveth me, shall be loved of my Father: and I will love him, and will manifest myself to him. 22 **Judas saith to him, not the Iscariot: Lord, how is it, that thou wilt manifest thyself to us, and not to the world?** 23 **Jesus answered, and said to him: If any one love me, he will keep my word, and my Father will love him, and we will come to him, and will make our abode with him.** 24 He that loveth me not, keepeth not my words. And the word which you have heard, is not mine; but the Father's who sent me. 25 These things have I spoken to you, abiding with you.

26 But the Paraclete, the Holy Ghost, whom the Father will send in my name, he will teach you all things, and bring all things to your mind, whatsoever I shall have said to you. 27 **Peace I leave with you, my peace I give unto you: not as the world giveth, do I give unto you.** Let not your heart be troubled, nor let it be afraid. 28 You have heard that I said to you: I go away, and I come unto you. **If you loved me, you would indeed be glad, because I go to the Father: for the Father is greater than I.** 29 And now I have told you before it come to pass: that when it shall come to pass, you may believe. 30 I will not now speak many things with you. **For the prince of this world cometh, and in me he hath not any thing.**

31 But that the world may know, that I love the Father: and as the Father hath given me commandment, so do I: Arise, let us go hence.

Reading with St. Augustine

"When the disciples ask questions and Jesus answers them as their teacher, when we read or listen to the Holy Gospel, we too learn as though we were with them," Augustine says. Saint Jude asks how Jesus will manifest Himself to the disciples and not to the world. Augustine, reading these words, answers in the same Holy Spirit, the same Paraclete, of Whom Jesus speaks: love distinguishes the saints from the world, because the Father and the Son make Their dwelling in a house united in love (see *Homilies* 76.1–2).

Christ speaks of a double peace for His disciples: peace in this world, so that we may love one another without judging hidden things, and peace in the world to come, where we have overcome our enemy. The prince of this world is the prince only of darkness (see *Homilies* 77.3; 79.2).

Christ speaks of another place for Himself and His disciples. As the Son of God, Jesus is always and already in heaven; Jesus speaks of bringing His human Flesh to the Father, to make it immortal. This is our joy, to live forever in the nature God has made us (see *Homilies* 78.3).

MEDITATIO

The upper room seemed still, yet charged with something greater than the disciples could grasp. Jesus's voice was steady: *"If you love Me, keep My commandments. And I will ask the Father, and He shall give you another Paraclete, that He may abide with you for ever."*

The disciples listened, uncertain yet hopeful. The Paraclete—*"advocate, comforter"*—would come to strengthen and guide them. Jesus promised that the Holy Spirit would *"teach you all things"* and remind them of His words. They did not fully understand, but their hearts stirred with longing.

St. Augustine states that the disciples' very questions at the Last Supper—Thomas asking about the way, Jude about Jesus's manifestation—were already prompted by the Spirit at work in them. They were asking as Apostles of Christ's Church. Their search was ours, too; their learning, our learning.

"Peace I leave with you, My peace I give unto you." Jesus's departure was not abandonment but fulfillment. His Flesh would leave them, ascending to the Father, but His Spirit would dwell within them—binding them into one Body, the Church.

Augustine sees in this a mystery of divine presence. On earth, Jesus remained united with the Father; now the Church, His living Body, remains united with Christ in heaven. Each member receives gifts in measure, but together, filled with the Spirit, the Church holds the *"immeasurable life of God."*

"Arise, let us go hence." His words echoed with purpose. Darkness loomed, but the prince of this world held no power over Him—or over those sealed with His Spirit. In that promised peace, they—and we—find courage, even in the face of the coming night.

ORATIO

1. John the Evangelist, who begins his gospel in the heights of heaven, lifts us again to lofty themes. We should not be afraid of confronting deep theological truth, because the Holy Spirit is with us. Let me imagine I am at the Last Supper with Jesus; what question do I want to ask Him?

2. John's gospel, like the other gospels, also confronts us with the gritty details of Jesus's earthly life. Let me bring to mind some aspect of my earthly life that weighs on me and bring that suffering or simple annoyance to my contemplation of heavenly things.

3. Where do I most feel at peace in the Church and in this world? How does this anticipate life in the world to come?

CONTEMPLATIO

LECTIO: JOHN 15:1–12

Subject: Joined in Love

1 **I am the true vine; and my Father is the husbandman.** 2 Every branch in me, that beareth not fruit, he will take away: and every one that beareth fruit, he will purge it, that it may bring forth more fruit. 3 **Now you are clean by reason of the word, which I have spoken to you.** 4 Abide in me, and I in you. As the branch cannot bear fruit of itself, unless it abide in the vine, so neither can you, unless you abide in me. 5 I am the vine; you the branches: he that abideth in me, and I in him, the same beareth much fruit: for **without me you can do nothing.**

6 If any one abide not in me, he shall be cast forth as a branch, and shall wither, and they shall gather him up, and cast him into the fire, and he burneth. 7 If you abide in me, and my words abide in you, you shall ask whatever you will, and it shall be done unto you. 8 In this is my Father glorified; that you bring forth very much fruit, and become my disciples. 9 As the Father hath loved me, I also have loved you. Abide in my love. 10 **If you keep my commandments, you shall abide in my love; as I also have kept my Father's commandments, and do abide in his love.**

11 These things I have spoken to you, that my joy may be in you, and your joy may be filled. 12 **This is my commandment, that you love one another, as I have loved you.**

Reading with St. Augustine

Augustine clears up what seems to be a conundrum, in Christ's identifying Himself as the vine and the Father as the vine grower (husbandman): Christ is God, so He is both vine and pruner. Christ shows Himself the pruner by declaring that His disciples are clean by the word He has spoken (see *Homilies* 80.2).

Augustine paraphrases Jesus's expression, "For without me you can do nothing," by asking, "What in fact is man apart from the fact that God took him up?" All of our spiritual merit begins with the Word taking Flesh, with the divine Son of God taking on our human nature (*Homilies* 82.4).

"Where there's charity, therefore, what is there that could be missing?" Augustine says. Belief does not necessarily produce love; demons believe but do not love. Yet even when we love our neighbor, love for God is there (*Homilies* 83.3).

MEDITATIO

On His way to the Garden of Gethesemane, Jesus spoke, *"I am the true vine, and My Father is the husbandman."* The disciples listened, their minds turning to familiar vineyards clinging to rocky hillsides, their roots stubbornly seeking life.

"Abide in Me, and I in you. As the branch cannot bear fruit of itself, except it abide in the vine, so neither can you, unless you abide in Me." His voice was steady but urgent—a call to remain connected, to live not by their strength but by His life flowing through them. There is no aspect of our life, from our creation to our salvation, in which we are not completely and continually dependent on God.

In Christ we *"live, and move, and are"* (see (Acts 17:28). Cut off from the vine, the branch withers and dies, fit only for fire. So, too, are our souls apart from God—created by love, yet lifeless without His grace.

"As the Father hath loved Me, I also have loved you. Abide in My love." Jesus's command was simple yet profound: live in love. It was the same love that bound Him to the Father—a love poured out even unto death.

John is never shy of recording Jesus's warnings, and Jesus reminds His disciples that it is possible for them to separate themselves from God, just as our first parents have done. The wood of a grapevine is not good for anything else if it is not joined to the root and stock. Our deeds mean nothing if we do not do them in love, yet the littlest deeds we do in love mean everything.

ORATIO

1. We Christians must always be evaluating our words and deeds according to the motive of love. One way of doing this is to ask whether our actions separate us from the Church and her teaching.

2. Another way to evaluate our love is to ask where our actions lead us: to our own pleasure, to making others dependent on us, or to filling our neighbor with love for God.

CONTEMPLATIO

LECTIO: JOHN 15:13–27

Subject: Friendship in Life and Death

13 Greater love than this no man hath, that a man lay down his
life for his friends. 14 You are my friends, if you do the things
that I command you. 15 **I will not now call you servants: for
the servant knoweth not what his lord doth. But I have called
you friends: because all things whatsoever I have heard of my
Father, I have made known to you.**

16 **You have not chosen me: but I have chosen you; and
have appointed you, that you should go, and should bring
forth fruit; and your fruit should remain:** that whatsoever you
shall ask of the Father in my name, he may give it you. 17 These
things I command you, that you love one another. 18 If the world
hate you, know ye, that it hath hated me before you. **19 If you had
been of the world, the world would love its own: but because
you are not of the world, but I have chosen you out of the
world, therefore the world hateth you.** 20 Remember my word
that I said to you: The servant is not greater than his master. If they
have persecuted me, they will also persecute you: if they have kept
my word, they will keep yours also.

21 But all these things they will do to you for my name's sake:
because they know not him that sent me. 22 If I had not come, and
spoken to them, they would not have sin; but now they have no
excuse for their sin. 23 He that hateth me, hateth my Father also.
24 If I had not done among them the works that no other man
hath done, they would not have sin; but now they have both seen
and hated both me and my Father. 25 But that the word may be
fulfilled which is written in their law: *They hated me without cause.*

26 But when the Paraclete cometh, whom I will send you from
the Father, the Spirit of truth, who proceedeth from the Father,
he shall give testimony of me. 27 And you shall give testimony,
because you are with me from the beginning.

Reading with St. Augustine

Augustine, reflecting on servitude and friendship, tells us there are two kinds of fear, which produce two kinds of servitude: there is a servile fear, a fear of punishment, which perfect love casts out (see 1 Jn. 4:18), from which Jesus is releasing His disciples by calling them friends; there is also a chaste fear, in which a servant looks forward to his master's joy and seeks to please him (see *Homilies* 85.3).

"[Christ] doesn't choose the good but rather makes good those whom he chooses," Augustine says. The good gives birth to love. Christ has made us good in His love, so we should bear the fruit of love (*Homilies* 86.3).

"The world is those who hate us," Augustine says, and he goes on to describe the confusion of human loves and hate by which the world wraps itself in darkness. The world hates those whom it punishes for crimes and it loves those who are its partners in crime (*Homilies* 87.4; 88.4).

MEDITATIO

Jesus speaks solemnly to the Apostles: *"Greater love than this no man hath, that a man lay down his life for his friends."* These words are to be their lodestar, and ours, guiding us through the world's thick tangle of love and hate. The world celebrates those who accomplish great feats of art, science, and politics, and turns on them overnight when it is convenient to find some criminal to convict or some celebrity to cancel. The world does the same to Jesus, loving Him for His miracles and then killing Him at the instigation of the authorities who are jealous of their position. Jesus offers us His friendship as our way out of the world of hate.

Friendship means equality with Christ, not the fearful servitude of a distant God. Friends serve one another out of love. Friends help, friends give, friends love without seeking payback. This is the chaste fear of which Augustine speaks, which serves without taking anything from the beloved. Our friendship with Christ urges us to share the sacrifice He makes for us. We may suffer and even be killed for Him, the way many martyrs have been throughout the world. Augustine reminds us that true martyrdom happens only when we suffer for God, not for personal grievance. The world's hatred may cancel reputations or destroy lives, but it cannot erase the friendship Christ offers. In laying down our lives—whether through daily sacrifice or ultimate martyrdom—we abide in His love, where no worldly power can reach. *"I have chosen you,"* Jesus said. *"That you should go, and bring forth fruit."*

ORATIO

1. Jesus is preparing His disciples for the persecution that will erupt after His resurrection. Have I faced persecution for my Christian faith? Have I responded with hate or with love?

2. Are there ways in which I let the world move my feelings of love and hate? Have I judged any person near or far from me based on what others have said about him?

3. What remains of servile fear in my relationship with Christ? What would it take to make me feel fully friends with Him?

CONTEMPLATIO

LECTIO: JOHN 16:1–15

Subject: Better Knowing through the Spirit

1 These things have I spoken to you, that you may not be scandalized. 2 They will put you out of the synagogues: yea, the hour cometh, that whosoever killeth you, will think that he doth a service to God. 3 And these things will they do to you; because they have not known the Father, nor me. 4 But these things I have told you, that when the hour shall come, you may remember that I told you of them. 5 But I told you not these things from the beginning, because I was with you. And now I go to him that sent me, and none of you asketh me: Whither goest thou?

6 But because I have spoken these things to you, sorrow hath filled your heart. 7 **But I tell you the truth: it is expedient to you that I go: for if I go not, the Paraclete will not come to you; but if I go, I will send him to you.** 8 And when he is come, he will convince the world of sin, and of justice, and of judgment. 9 Of sin: because they believed not in me. 10 And of justice: because I go to the Father; and you shall see me no longer.

11 And of judgment: because the prince of this world is already judged. 12 I have yet many things to say to you: but you cannot bear them now. 13 **But when he, the Spirit of truth, is come, he will teach you all truth.** For he shall not speak of himself; but what things soever he shall hear, he shall speak; and the things that are to come, he shall shew you. 14 He shall glorify me; because he shall receive of mine, and shall shew it to you. 15 All things whatsoever the Father hath, are mine. Therefore I said, that he shall receive of mine, and shew it to you.

Reading with St. Augustine

Augustine tells us that we do not love what we do not know and that once we love something about which we know even a little, that love leads us to know the thing better and more fully. It is in this love that the Holy Spirit teaches the Church all truth (see *Homilies* 96.4).

Christ, Whom the disciples love, must be taken from their sight so that they can know Him in a spiritual way. In fact, Augustine says, once the Holy Spirit comes, even the apostles no longer know Christ's Flesh according to the flesh, but according to spiritual knowledge (see *Homilies* 94.4).

Knowledge of Christ in the Flesh, including His Cross, death, and resurrection, is the genuine milk of spiritual knowledge, from which Christ weans His disciples when He is taken up in glory. The Holy Spirit feeds spiritual persons with solid food, knowledge of Christ as God. Augustine advises us that these forms of knowledge are not opposed to each other any more than a building is opposed to the foundation on which it stands: "Hence, little ones shouldn't be suckled to such a degree that they never understand that Christ is God, nor should they be weaned in such a way that they leave behind Christ the man" (*Homilies* 98.6).

MEDITATIO

Jesus continues to form his Apostles, stating, *"When the Paraclete cometh, the Spirit of truth . . . He shall guide you into all truth."* His words were both a promise and a preparation. The disciples, still uncertain, listened with hearts torn between hope and fear.

St. Augustine reflects that love itself leads to deeper understanding. Just as a child drawn to art or science devotes herself to learning, or two lovers move from attraction to profound union, so too does love for Christ draw the soul into ever-deepening knowledge of God. We cannot love what we do not know. Love bridges the gap between what we see and know and what we cannot yet comprehend.

Jesus was preparing His disciples for a love that would demand everything. *"It is expedient for you that I go,"* He told them. Only through His departure could the Holy Spirit come to guide them—not as learners still clinging to earthly familiarity, but as spiritual adults called to transform the world.

"He shall glorify Me, because He shall receive of Mine." The Spirit would illuminate everything Jesus taught, binding heaven and earth through love's perfect knowledge.

Augustine reminds us that every first love reshapes our world. Christ's commandment of love—love of God and neighbor—becomes the measure of all things. What fits remains; what doesn't must fall away. The Spirit teaches this love, leading us into truth, sanctifying even our struggles.

Jesus was about to consummate His love on the Cross, offering everything. His disciples, guided by the Spirit, would follow. So must we, letting love guide us—through fear, through loss—until we are one with the God who first loved us.

ORATIO

1. What is my state in life—single, married, widowed, consecrated, ordained? Let me relive, with gratitude to God, the form that love and knowledge have taken in reaching this state.

2. Has my state of life broken down in any way? With the help of the Holy Spirit, let me convict myself of sin, injustice, and judgment, confident that my loving Christ can repair all within me and outside of me.

3. Do I tend to focus more on Christ the man or Christ as God? Let me balance out my knowledge of Christ by loving, through meditation, some aspect of Him I have neglected.

CONTEMPLATIO

LECTIO: JOHN 16:16–33

Subject: Action Following Contemplation

[16] A little while, and now you shall not see me; and again a little while, and you shall see me: because I go to the Father. [17] Then some of his disciples said one to another: What is this that he saith to us: A little while, and you shall not see me; and again a little while, and you shall see me, and, because I go to the Father? [18] They said therefore: What is this that he saith, A little while? we know not what he speaketh. [19] **And Jesus knew that they had a mind to ask him**; and he said to them: Of this do you inquire among yourselves, because I said: A little while, and you shall not see me; and again a little while, and you shall see me? [20] Amen, amen I say to you, that you shall lament and weep, but the world shall rejoice; and you shall be made sorrowful, but your sorrow shall be turned into joy.

[21] **A woman, when she is in labour, hath sorrow, because her hour is come; but when she hath brought forth the child, she remembereth no more the anguish, for joy that a man is born into the world.** [22] So also you now indeed have sorrow; but I will see you again, and your heart shall rejoice; and your joy no man shall take from you. [23] And in that day you shall not ask me any thing. **Amen, amen I say to you: if you ask the Father any thing in my name, he will give it you.** [24] Hitherto you have not asked any thing in my name. Ask, and you shall receive; that your joy may be full. [25] These things I have spoken to you in proverbs. The hour cometh, when I will no more speak to you in proverbs, but will shew you plainly of the Father.

[26] In that day you shall ask in my name; and I say not to you, that I will ask the Father for you: [27] For the Father himself loveth you, because you have loved me, and have believed that I came out from God. [28] I came forth from the Father, and am come into the world: again I leave the world, and I go to the Father. [29] His disciples say to him: Behold, now thou speakest plainly, and speakest no proverb. [30] **Now we know that thou knowest all things, and thou needest not that any man should ask thee.** By this we believe that thou camest forth from God.

[31] Jesus answered them: Do you now believe? [32] Behold, the hour cometh, and it is now come, that you shall be scattered every

man to his own, and shall leave me alone; and yet I am not alone, because the Father is with me. [33] These things I have spoken to you, that in me you may have peace. In the world you shall have distress: but have confidence, I have overcome the world.

Reading with St. Augustine

Human beings in a position of knowledge need their students to ask them questions so they know what response to give, but in the case of Christ, Who knows everything, He puts up with questions for the sake of revealing the hearts of those around Him and showing us the best ways to approach Him ourselves (see *Homilies* 103.2).

Jesus instructs His disciples to ask in His name, and Augustine specifies that this is not simply to add certain sounds and syllables to our prayer but to ask for what is in keeping with our salvation: "Whatever is asked for that isn't in keeping with salvation isn't asked for in the Savior's name" (*Homilies* 102.1).

The Church is the woman in labor, groaning in her desire to see God. The Church travails in the current age in order to lead all her members to the contemplation of God (see *Homilies* 101.5).

MEDITATIO

Jesus spoke His final words before the start of his Passion, *"A little while, and you shall not see Me . . . and again a little while, and you shall see Me."* His disciples struggled to understand, their minds fixed on immediate concerns, on what might happen next.

St. Augustine sees this moment as a call to contemplation in the face of action. The world prizes action—building, providing, securing justice. These are good and necessary things, but they are not life's ultimate purpose. Augustine, a bishop in chaotic times, knew this well. His life was marked by both tireless work and profound contemplation. His deepest insights flowed not from ceaseless action but from silent prayer and meditation on God's truth.

Jesus, too, shows that true power comes from contemplation of the Father. *"I am not alone, because the Father is with Me."* His strength for the Cross, His ability to endure betrayal, suffering, and death—all comes from His divine and perfect union with the Father.

"These things I have spoken to you, that in Me you may have peace." Jesus urged His disciples toward peace—not the world's fleeting peace, but the lasting peace found in communion with God.

"In the world you shall have distress: but have confidence, I have overcome the world." When the world moves in frenzied opposition to Christ, His followers must act—but first, they must pray, meditate, and contemplate. They must anchor themselves in the One who has already conquered. There is a spiritual priority to the interior life.

ORATIO

1. How has my private prayer and meditation on Scripture guided, enhanced, and perfected my work in the world?

2. Have prayer and meditation shaped the way I ask the Lord for things?

3. What does contemplation feel like for me right now? What do I imagine it to be in the world to come?

CONTEMPLATIO

LECTIO: JOHN 17:1–11

Subject: Knowledge of God in Life and Death

[1] **These things Jesus spoke, and lifting up his eyes to heaven,
he said: Father, the hour is come, glorify thy Son, that thy Son
may glorify thee.** [2] As thou hast given him power over all flesh,
that he may give eternal life to all whom thou hast given him.
[3] Now this is eternal life: That they may know thee, the only true
God, and Jesus Christ, whom thou hast sent. [4] **I have glorified
thee on the earth; I have finished the work which thou gavest
me to do.** [5] And now glorify thou me, O Father, with thyself, with
the glory which I had, before the world was, with thee.

[6] I have manifested thy name to the men whom thou hast giv-
en me out of the world. **Thine they were, and to me thou gavest
them; and they have kept thy word.** [7] Now they have known,
that all things which thou hast given me, are from thee: [8] Because
the words which thou gavest me, I have given to them; and they
have received them, and have known in very deed that I came out
from thee, and they have believed that thou didst send me. [9] I pray
for them: I pray not for the world, but for them whom thou hast
given me: because they are thine: [10] **And all my things are thine,
and thine are mine; and I am glorified in them.**

[11] And now I am not in the world, and these are in the world,
and I come to thee. Holy Father, keep them in thy name whom
thou hast given me; that they may be one, as we also are.

Reading with St. Augustine

Augustine reminds us, once again, that everything Jesus says, He says for our sake as our teacher, including this prayer to the Father. When Jesus prays, "Glorify thy Son," He is demonstrating that all He has done and is about to undergo is subject to God alone and no other force (see *Homilies* 104.2).

The glory of God on earth is knowledge of God; Jesus has glorified God this way. The glory of God is complete in heaven because our knowledge of Him is complete only there (see *Homilies* 105.3).

Augustine, reflecting on the gift God makes of us to Jesus, acknowledges that, as the Son of God, everything the Father possesses belongs also to the Son in eternity. The disciples now belong to Jesus in the flesh (see *Homilies* 106.5).

MEDITATIO

Still in intimate conversation with his Apostles, Christ looks upwards and petitions, *"Father, the hour is come. Glorify Thy Son, that Thy Son may glorify Thee."* His voice was steady, filled with purpose. The Apostles, gathered around Him, listened in awe. This was no ordinary prayer—it was an unveiling of eternity.

St. Augustine reflects that in this moment, Jesus allows us to glimpse the inner life of God—the infinite love exchanged between Father and Son. This love, perfect and eternal, now reaches into the world, drawing humanity into its divine embrace.

"This is eternal life: that they may know Thee, the only true God, and Jesus Christ, whom Thou hast sent." Life itself is defined not by what we achieve or possess, but by knowing God—by being in communion with Him.

"They were Thine, and Thou hast given them to Me." Jesus sees His disciples, weak and uncertain, as precious gifts from the Father. He prays not to escape suffering but to lift His friends into the very heart of God's love.

The world's way of facing death is practical—settling affairs, making plans. But Jesus does something infinitely greater: He prepares His Apostles by raising their minds to heaven and the ultimate goal of doing the Father's will. He prays for unity, for them to be one as He and the Father are one—a unity sealed by the Cross.

In that prayer, we find our truest identity—not as isolated souls, but as God's gift, loved and cherished, called into the eternal life of the Trinity. In Him, even suffering becomes glory.

ORATIO

1. Have I imagined my own death? Have I come close to death before? What would I want it to look like?

2. Have I imagined heaven, eternal life with God? What do I want it to look like?

3. Let me meditate on my own being as a gift from Father to Son and from Son to Father.

CONTEMPLATIO

LECTIO: JOHN 17:12–26

Subject: Our Eternal Possession

12 While I was with them, I kept them in thy name. Those whom thou gavest me have I kept; and none of them is lost, but the son of perdition, that the scripture may be fulfilled. 13 And now I come to thee; and these things I speak in the world, that they may have my joy filled in themselves. 14 I have given them thy word, and the world hath hated them, because they are not of the world; as I also am not of the world. 15 I pray not that thou shouldst take them out of the world, but that thou shouldst keep them from evil.

16 They are not of the world, as I also am not of the world. 17 Sanctify them in truth. Thy word is truth. 18 As thou hast sent me into the world, I also have sent them into the world. 19 And for them do I sanctify myself, that they also may be sanctified in truth. 20 **And not for them only do I pray, but for them also who through their word shall believe in me;**

21 That they all may be one, as thou, Father, in me, and I in thee; that they also may be one in us; that the world may believe that thou hast sent me. 22 And the glory which thou hast given me, I have given to them; that they may be one, as we also are one: 23 I in them, and thou in me; that they may be made perfect in one: and the world may know that thou hast sent me, and hast loved them, as thou hast also loved me. 24 **Father, I will that where I am, they also whom thou hast given me may be with me; that they may see my glory which thou hast given me, because thou hast loved me before the creation of the world.** 25 Just Father, the world hath not known thee; but I have known thee: and these have known that thou hast sent me.

26 And I have made known thy name to them, and will make it known; that the love wherewith thou hast loved me, may be in them, and I in them.

Reading with St. Augustine

Augustine shows us ourselves in Jesus's prayer: "And so not only those are to be understood who he said were going to believe in him through their word, who heard the apostles themselves when they were living in the flesh, but also those [who came] after their death. We too, who were born much later, have also believed in

Christ through their word, because those who were with him at that time preached to the others what they heard from him, and thus their word came all the way to us, so that we too, everywhere that his Church is, would believe, and it is going to come to those further on, whoever and wherever they may be, who will eventually believe in him" (*Homilies* 109.1).

Augustine points our gaze in the same direction Christ is praying: "The Lord Jesus lifts his followers up to so great a hope that there can be none greater. Listen, and be joyful in the hope on whose account this life isn't to be loved but endured, so that you may be patient in its tribulation. Listen, I say, and attend to where our hope is being lifted. . . . Listen, believe, hope, desire what he tells of: *Father*, he says, *I wish that those whom you gave me would also be with me where I am* (John 17:24)" (*Homilies* 111.1).

MEDITATIO

Knowing his Passion would begin at the conclusion of his prayer to the Father, Jesus said: *"Father, I will that where I am, they also whom Thou hast given Me may be with Me."* His words carried the weight of eternity, echoing not just through the upper room but across all time.

St. Augustine reminds us that Christ's prayer is timeless. Though spoken on the eve of His Passion, these words reach into every age, calling each of us into the heart of God's love. Jesus prayed not only for His disciples then, but for all who would believe in Him through their witness—including us.

"Those whom Thou gavest Me have I kept." Even in the coming darkness, when betrayal and fear would scatter His friends, His love remained constant. He prayed not for escape from suffering, but for unity—*"that they may be one, as We also are."*

After the Cross, in the stillness of Holy Saturday, we can imagine John remembering these words, perhaps even writing them down. He alone stood at the foot of the Cross; he alone saw the fullness of Jesus's love poured out. Those words must have burned within him: *"Thou hast loved them, as Thou hast loved Me."*

For John, for Augustine, and for us, this prayer is a beacon through life's trials. It draws us into contemplation, lifting our hearts beyond earthly suffering toward Christ's eternal glory. Our contemplation of Christ, aided by meditating on Scripture and sharing in the priestly prayer at the altar, is our light until our time on earth comes to a close.

ORATIO

1. Let me meditate on Christ's desire to have me with Him forever.

CONTEMPLATIO

LECTIO: JOHN 18:1–14

Subject: Right Action before Christ

[1] When Jesus had said these things, he went forth with his disciples over the brook Cedron, where there was a garden, into which he entered with his disciples. [2] And Judas also, who betrayed him, knew the place; because Jesus had often resorted thither together with his disciples. [3] Judas therefore having received a band of soldiers and servants from the chief priests and the Pharisees, cometh thither with lanterns and torches and weapons. [4] Jesus therefore, knowing all things that should come upon him, went forth, and said to them: Whom seek ye? [5] They answered him: Jesus of Nazareth. Jesus saith to them: I am he. And Judas also, who betrayed him, stood with them.

[6] **As soon therefore as he had said to them: I am he; they went backward, and fell to the ground.** [7] Again therefore he asked them: Whom seek ye? And they said: Jesus of Nazareth. [8] Jesus answered: I have told you that I am he. If therefore you seek me, let these go their way, [9] That the word might be fulfilled which he said: Of them whom thou hast given me, I have not lost any one. [10] **Then Simon Peter, having a sword, drew it, and struck the servant of the high priest, and cut off his right ear. And the name of the servant was Malchus.**

[11] Jesus therefore said to Peter: Put up thy sword into the scabbard. The chalice which my Father hath given me, shall I not drink it? [12] Then the band and the tribune, and the servants of the Jews, took Jesus, and bound him: [13] And they led him away to Annas first, for he was father in law to Caiphas, who was the high priest of that year. [14] Now Caiphas was he who had given the counsel to the Jews: That it was expedient that one man should die for the people.

Reading with St. Augustine

Augustine sees a spiritual meaning in all that happens around Christ, including the details of His trial. In those who fall backward to the ground at Jesus's proclamation, "I am he," Augustine sees those among us who fall back from our true and heavenly Christ for an earthly antichrist (see *Homilies* 112.3).

The soldiers do not seize Christ right away but fall backward to the ground to show that Jesus remains in full control of the situation. He is offering Himself freely (see *Homilies* 112.3).

Augustine interprets the name Malchus as "one who is going to reign." As a servant, he represents those in slavery to sin and the letter of the law, who are given a new ear to hear the newness of the Spirit and who will reign with Christ (see *Homilies* 112.5).

MEDITATIO

The stillness of Gethsemane shattered with the clash of steel and the shuffle of approaching soldiers. Torches flared, casting harsh light on the olive trees as Jesus stepped forward with calm authority: *"Whom seek ye?"*.

"Jesus of Nazareth," they answered.

"I am He." Jesus responded calmly. Even in surrender, Jesus's divine majesty could not be concealed.

Amid the chaos, Peter lunged forward, drawing his sword with reckless zeal. His blade found Malchus, the high priest's servant, slashing his ear. Peter thought he was defending Christ, but Jesus needed no defense.

"Put up thy sword into the scabbard." His tone was resolute yet merciful. Peter's act of violence could not hinder the divine plan. Turning to Malchus, Jesus reached out and healed the wound, restoring what Peter had tried to take away (Luke 22:51). Malchus, drawn there by duty, became a witness to unexpected grace.

Augustine sees in Malchus a symbol of those in slavery to sin, unaware of their need for spiritual healing. When Jesus heals his ear, he opens Malchus's heart.

The first thing Malchus hears with new ears of faith is Jesus's determination to die for us sinners: *"The chalice which My Father hath given Me, shall I not drink it?"* Jesus's surrender was deliberate, His love unwavering. In that moment, He stood alone—yet He held every wounded soul in His mercy, offering not resistance but redemption. Even Malchus, even us.

ORATIO

1. Let me put myself in the place of Malchus. How well do I understand the situation in which I serve the high priest? This Jesus has just healed me, and now I lead Him away for trial. What is in my heart and mind?

2. I see soldiers falling to the ground at Jesus's declaration, "I am he." They seek to serve the false christ of the world, not the true Christ. In what ways do I continue to stumble and fall at what Jesus Christ is asking of me?

3. Let me put myself in the place of Peter. I stand with my sword in my hand. It drips with blood spilled futilely while I watch the soldiers lead my Lord away.

CONTEMPLATIO

LECTIO: JOHN 18:15–27

Subject: Where I Stand before Christ

[15] And Simon Peter followed Jesus, and so did another disciple. And that disciple was known to the high priest, and went in with Jesus into the court of the high priest. [16] But Peter stood at the door without. The other disciple therefore, who was known to the high priest, went out, and spoke to the portress, and brought in Peter. [17] **The maid therefore that was portress, saith to Peter: Art not thou also one of this man's disciples? He saith: I am not.** [18] Now the servants and ministers stood at a fire of coals, because it was cold, and warmed themselves. And with them was Peter also, standing, and warming himself. [19] The high priest therefore asked Jesus of his disciples, and of his doctrine. [20] Jesus answered him: I have spoken openly to the world: I have always taught in the synagogue, and in the temple, whither all the Jews resort; and in secret I have spoken nothing.

[21] Why askest thou me? ask them who have heard what I have spoken unto them: behold they know what things I have said. [22] **And when he had said these things, one of the servants standing by, gave Jesus a blow, saying: Answerest thou the high priest so?** [23] **Jesus answered him: If I have spoken evil, give testimony of the evil; but if well, why strikest thou me?** [24] And Annas sent him bound to Caiphas the high priest. [25] **And Simon Peter was standing, and warming himself. They said therefore to him: Art not thou also one of his disciples? He denied it, and said: I am not.**

[26] **One of the servants of the high priest (a kinsman to him whose ear Peter cut off) saith to him: Did not I see thee in the garden with him?** [27] **Again therefore Peter denied; and immediately the cock crew.**

Reading with St. Augustine

Augustine tells us that in denying Christ, Peter has denied being a Christian as well: "The one who has denied that he is Christ's disciple, then, has denied the very thing that goes by the title of Christian" (*Homilies* 113.2).

Christ, though, anticipating this denial, tells the soldiers to let His disciples go free (see John 18:8). This gives Peter the freedom both to deny Christ; that is, to sin, and yet not to be cut off immediately forever: "If Peter left at that moment after having denied Christ, what else would he have been but lost?" (*Homilies* 113.2).

In considering Jesus's reply to being struck on the cheek, Augustine asks why Jesus does not simply turn the other cheek (see Matt. 5:39). Augustine says that Jesus did: "He responded truthfully, meekly and righteously." After all, "It can happen that an angry person, too, would be demonstrative in offering his other cheek. How much better is it, then, both to respond peacefully with the truth and to be ready to endure worse things with a tranquil mind!" (*Homilies* 113.4).

MEDITATIO

The courtyard flickered with firelight as Peter hovered near the glowing coals, hands stretched toward their warmth. The chill of the night was nothing compared to the cold fear gripping his heart. He had followed Jesus—but at a distance, afraid to be seen, afraid to be known.

Inside, Jesus stood bound before the high priest. When struck by a servant, He did not resist, did not retaliate. His calm reply echoed through the hall: *"If I have spoken evil, give testimony of the evil; but if well, why strikest thou Me?"* There was no anger, only unwavering truth.

Peter watched from the shadows, torn between love and fear. A servant girl's accusing voice pierced the night: *"Art not thou also one of this man's disciples?"* Peter recoiled: *"I am not."*

St. Augustine reflects that Peter, clinging to the fire's warmth, sought comfort in what could not save him. He had acted boldly in the garden but now shrank back, afraid of being caught in Jesus's fate.

Two more times the question came, and two more times Peter denied. Then, the cock crowed—a sharp, accusing sound that shattered his defenses. He remembered Jesus's words, *"Before the cock crow, thou shalt deny Me thrice."*

Peter was one step from the outer darkness, yet grace was already reaching for him. The same Christ he denied would soon turn and look upon him—not with condemnation, but with mercy that would burn deeper than any fire, restoring him through repentance and love.

ORATIO

1. Let me challenge myself as a Christian. Where am I in this scene? Am I Christ, submitting to unreasonable inquiry and even violence, and doing so patiently, truthfully, and meekly? Or do I turn the other cheek in anger, to prove my point and show myself righteous in my own eyes? Am I the disciple who has enough courage to follow Jesus into the courtyard of the high priest, to stand and watch and learn from Jesus? Am I Peter, who limits his Christian witness to mere curiosity, who enjoys the comforts of this world while at a distance from suffering, who is one step away from the outer darkness by denying the core of my faith?

CONTEMPLATIO

LECTIO: JOHN 18:28–40

Subject: Contemplation against Malice and Madness

28 **Then they led Jesus from Caiphas to the governor's hall.**
And it was morning; and they went not into the hall, that they
might not be defiled, but that they might eat the pasch. 29 Pilate
therefore went out to them, and said: What accusation bring you
against this man? 30 They answered, and said to him: If he were not
a malefactor, we would not have delivered him up to thee.

31 Pilate therefore said to them: Take him you, and judge him
according to your law. The Jews therefore said to him: It is not
lawful for us to put any man to death; 32 That the word of Jesus
might be fulfilled, which he said, signifying what death he should
die. 33 Pilate therefore went into the hall again, and called Jesus,
and said to him: Art thou the king of the Jews? 34 Jesus answered:
Sayest thou this thing of thyself, or have others told it thee of me?
35 Pilate answered: Am I a Jew? Thy own nation, and the chief
priests, have delivered thee up to me: what hast thou done?

36 Jesus answered: My kingdom is not of this world. If my
kingdom were of this world, my servants would certainly strive
that I should not be delivered to the Jews: but now my kingdom
is not from hence. 37 Pilate therefore said to him: Art thou a king
then? **Jesus answered: Thou sayest that I am a king. For this was**
I born, and for this came I into the world; that I should give
testimony to the truth. Every one that is of the truth, heareth
my voice. 38 **Pilate saith to him: What is truth? And when he**
said this, he went out again to the Jews, and saith to them: I
find no cause in him. 39 **But you have a custom that I should**
release one unto you at the pasch: will you, therefore, that I re-
lease unto you the king of the Jews? 40 Then cried they all again,
saying: Not this man, but Barabbas. Now Barabbas was a robber.

Reading with St. Augustine

Augustine lays out the hypocrisy of those who hand Jesus over to the Romans for trial: "Have you grown so hardened, false Israelites, have you become so senseless in your exceeding malice as to believe that you aren't polluted by innocent blood because you have handed him over to someone else who will shed it?" (*Homilies* 114.4).

The Romans, according to Augustine, are guilty of madness in acting as they do, with complicity (*Homilies* 114.5).

Augustine says that when Jesus responds to Pilate, "*Thou sayest* that I am a king," Jesus is telling Pilate, "You who are carnal are speaking carnally." Christ's kingdom is spiritual, and so neither the Jewish nor the Roman authorities have anything to fear. They should meditate on what truth is, which Pilate, in speaking of releasing a prisoner, distracts himself from doing (*Homilies* 115.2–5).

MEDITATIO

The early morning light fell coldly on the stone courtyard as Jesus was led into the praetorium. Outside, the religious authorities hovered, refusing to enter lest they become ritually unclean for the Passover—blind to the darkness already staining their souls. Their hands were clean of Roman contamination, but their hearts were steeped in envy and malice.

Inside, Pilate confronted a different challenge. *"Art Thou the King of the Jews?"* His tone was skeptical but searching. Jesus's answer shattered the narrow confines of politics: *"My kingdom is not of this world."*

Pilate's heart wavered, brushing against eternal truth—but the weight of power and public opinion pressed him down. *"What is truth?"* he asked, but he did not wait for an answer. Truth stood before him, silent yet commanding.

Seeking escape from responsibility, Pilate turned to problem-solving: *"Whom will you that I release to you—Barabbas, or Jesus?"* He chose expediency over contemplation, comfort over courage.

We, too, face Pilate's choice daily: cling to control, or open our hearts to the unsettling, life-altering truth of Christ. Pilate walked away—but the question remains, pressing into every soul: *"What is truth?"* Will we stand before it—or flee into the safety of shadows?

ORATIO

1. Jesus calls us to take up our cross and follow Him, to share in His passion. A good way to start is to place ourselves in the position of those who persecute Him. Have I abused or slandered those who act in the person of Christ for me—my deacons, priests, bishop, or pope, or anyone who teaches or leads in the Church?

2. Do I submit to distractions in prayer and meditation by trying to solve problems, as Pilate does, when God presents me with a chance to contemplate Him?

3. Jesus's kingdom is not of this world. What do I still want His kingdom to accomplish for me and for this world?

CONTEMPLATIO

LECTIO: JOHN 19:1–16

Subject: The Word of the Cross

1 Then therefore, Pilate took Jesus, and scourged him. 2 And the soldiers platting a crown of thorns, put it upon his head; and they put on him a purple garment. 3 And they came to him, and said: Hail, king of the Jews; and they gave him blows. 4 Pilate therefore went forth again, and saith to them: Behold, I bring him forth unto you, that you may know that I find no cause in him. 5 (Jesus therefore came forth, bearing the crown of thorns and the purple garment.) And he saith to them: Behold the Man.

6 When the chief priests, therefore, and the servants, had seen him, they cried out, saying: Crucify him, crucify him. Pilate saith to them: Take him you, and crucify him: for I find no cause in him. 7 The Jews answered him: We have a law; and according to the law he ought to die, because he made himself the Son of God. 8 When Pilate therefore had heard this saying, he feared the more. 9 And he entered into the hall again, and he said to Jesus: Whence art thou? **But Jesus gave him no answer.** 10 Pilate therefore saith to him: Speakest thou not to me? knowest thou not that I have power to crucify thee, and I have power to release thee?

11 Jesus answered: Thou shouldst not have any power against me, unless it were given thee from above. **Therefore, he that hath delivered me to thee, hath the greater sin.** 12 And from henceforth Pilate sought to release him. But the Jews cried out, saying: If thou release this man, thou art not Caesar's friend. For whosoever maketh himself a king, speaketh against Caesar. 13 Now when Pilate had heard these words, he brought Jesus forth, and sat down in the judgment seat, in the place that is called Lithostrotos, and in Hebrew Gabbatha. 14 And it was the parasceve of the pasch, about the sixth hour, and he saith to the Jews: Behold your king. 15 But they cried out: Away with him; away with him; crucify him. Pilate saith to them: Shall I crucify your king? The chief priests answered: We have no king but Caesar.

16 Then therefore he delivered him to them to be crucified. And they took Jesus, and led him forth.

Reading with St. Augustine

Augustine reflects on Jesus's silence before His accusers; He neither confirms nor denies their charge that He has declared Himself a king and Son of God. Both are true, of course, and as Augustine says, "Both would now have been shown forth were it not that, the more powerful he was, the more patient he preferred to be" (*Homilies* 116.3).

Even if the Jewish authorities, in handing Jesus over, have the "greater sin," Pilate is also guilty of sin (see *Homilies* 116.5).

MEDITATIO

Before the angry crowd stood Jesus, bruised and beaten, a crown of thorns pressed deep into His brow. *"Behold the man!"* Pilate declared, hoping the sight of such brutal humiliation would satisfy their thirst for vengeance.

But it did not. *"Crucify Him!"* they cried.

St. Augustine reflects that the Cross itself is a word—God's final, resounding proclamation to humanity. It speaks without syllables, its meaning etched in the tortured body of Christ. Human suffering always cries out, but when the suffering One is the eternal Word made Flesh, that cry becomes the language of salvation.

Pilate, trapped between fear and truth, wavered. He could not understand that Jesus's silence was not weakness but divine authority. *"Thou wouldst have no power against Me, unless it were given thee from above."* Power, stripped of truth, is illusion.

The Jewish authorities sinned by action—driven by envy and hatred, they demanded Jesus's death. Pilate sinned by omission—driven by cowardice, he yielded to their demands rather than defend the innocent. His question still echoes unanswered: *"What is truth?"*

Augustine reminds us that knowledge of God gives courage. But when knowledge falters, we have only to look upon the Cross. In its stark, wounded form lies every answer we need—truth spoken in suffering, love proven through sacrifice, and redemption offered without condition.

"Behold your King!" Pilate declared—but they turned away. We must choose whether to do the same—or let the Cross speak to us, transforming fear into faith and silence into eternal hope.

ORATIO

1. Let me imagine I am Pontius Pilate. What do I hear in Jesus's words, "Thou shouldst not have any power against me, unless it were given thee from above"?

2. What do I hear in Jesus's silence? How does His silence move me? What can I do to avoid sinning against the silent man before me?

CONTEMPLATIO

LECTIO: JOHN 19:17–30

Subject: Bringing My Gifts to the Cross with Mary

17 And bearing his own cross, he went forth to that place which is called Calvary, but in Hebrew Golgotha. 18 Where they crucified him, and with him two others, one on each side, and Jesus in the midst. 19 **And Pilate wrote a title also, and he put it upon the cross. And the writing was: JESUS OF NAZARETH, THE KING OF THE JEWS.** 20 This title therefore many of the Jews did read: because the place where Jesus was crucified was nigh to the city: and it was written in Hebrew, in Greek, and in Latin.

21 Then the chief priests of the Jews said to Pilate: Write not, The King of the Jews; but that he said, I am the King of the Jews. 22 Pilate answered: What I have written, I have written. 23 **The soldiers therefore, when they had crucified him, took his garments, (and they made four parts, to every soldier a part,)** and also his coat. Now the coat was without seam, woven from the top throughout. 24 They said then one to another: Let us not cut it, but let us cast lots for it, whose it shall be; that the scripture might be fulfilled, saying: *They have parted my garments among them, and upon my vesture they have cast lots.* And the soldiers indeed did these things. 25 Now there stood by the cross of Jesus, his mother, and his mother's sister, Mary of Cleophas, and Mary Magdalen.

26 **When Jesus therefore had seen his mother and the disciple standing whom he loved, he saith to his mother: Woman, behold thy son.** 27 **After that, he saith to the disciple: Behold thy mother. And from that hour, the disciple took her to his own.** 28 Afterwards, Jesus knowing that all things were now accomplished, that the scripture might be fulfilled, said: I thirst. 29 **Now there was a vessel set there full of vinegar. And they, putting a sponge full of vinegar about hyssop, put it to his mouth.** 30 Jesus therefore, when he had taken the vinegar, said: It is consummated. And bowing his head, he gave up the ghost.

Reading with St. Augustine

Augustine sees the inscription that Pilate has placed above Jesus, "Jesus of Nazareth, the King of the Jews," as referring to all Jews in spirit, the circumcision of the heart (see Rom. 2:29), and says that Pilate recognizes this, too (see *Homilies* 117.5).

Augustine reads in the casting of lots for Jesus's clothes and their division into four parts the giving of grace to the four corners of the world. It can seem like a lottery, the choice God makes among people from deep within His providence (see *Homilies* 118.4).

Whereas Jesus had said to Mary at the wedding in Cana that His hour had not yet come (see John 2:4), now He commends her: her gift to the world, the Flesh of Jesus, is now hanging on the Cross (see *Homilies* 119.1).

In the vinegar raised to Jesus's lips, Augustine sees those Jews who have degenerated from the wine of the patriarchs and prophets. In the hyssop, Augustine sees Jesus's humility, which is absorbed into the vinegar of wickedness. The reed used to raise the sponge is Scripture, which is being fulfilled (*Homilies* 119.4–5).

MEDITATIO

The hill of Calvary stood barren and bleak as Jesus carried His Cross, stumbling under its crushing weight. The soldiers led Him without mercy, His body already torn and bleeding. Yet, in that brutal march, the Cross was already speaking—declaring salvation through sacrifice.

St. Augustine sees the Cross as the living Word, proclaiming God's boundless love. Jesus held nothing back—not even His last earthly possession, His seamless tunic. The soldiers divided His garments into four parts, symbolizing the spread of the Gospel to the four corners of the world. Each received a portion, as we each receive different gifts from the Holy Spirit—determined not by chance but by God's perfect will.

Even Mary, standing at the foot of the Cross, participated in this mystery. She had given Jesus His human Flesh, the very Flesh now offered for the world's salvation. Augustine reflects that her role, though exalted, did not control His divine mission. Her place was not to command miracles but to witness the ultimate miracle—God's sacrifice of His Son.

"I thirst." They lifted vinegar to His lips—a bitter symbol of corrupted religion, of faith twisted for selfish gain. Augustine warns that we, too, offer vinegar to Christ when we use our faith to wound others or seek power.

Then came the final word: *"It is consummated."* The Cross spoke its last, transforming suffering into redemption, death into life. In that moment, the Word fulfilled its purpose—pouring out love without measure, offering salvation to the world.

ORATIO

1. When Mary stands before the Cross, she can see her own gift to the world, the Body of Christ, mocked and scorned. She does not feel sorrow for herself but for the One on the Cross, her Son, Jesus. Let me consider the gifts God has given me and how I may hang them upon the Cross with Christ.

2. I have inherited the rich wine of faith and good works from countless saints and holy ancestors. Let me thank God for this inheritance and ask Him where I risk letting it spoil into vinegar.

3. Let me imagine I am a soldier who takes some of Jesus's clothes. Is there anything that Jesus has given me that I hold onto for myself, for mere comfort in this world?

CONTEMPLATIO

LECTIO: JOHN 19:31–42

Subject: The Open Door and Sealed Tomb

31 Then the Jews, (because it was the parasceve,) that the bodies
might not remain upon the cross on the sabbath day, (for that was
a great sabbath day,) besought Pilate that their legs might be broken, and that they might be taken away. 32 The soldiers therefore
came; and they broke the legs of the first, and of the other that was
crucified with him. 33 But after they were come to Jesus, when they
saw that he was already dead, they did not break his legs. 34 **But
one of the soldiers with a spear opened his side, and immediately there came out blood and water.** 35 And he that saw it, hath
given testimony; and his testimony is true. And he knoweth that
he saith true; that you also may believe.

36 For these things were done, that the scripture might be
fulfilled: *You shall not break a bone of him.* 37 And again another
scripture saith: *They shall look on him whom they pierced.* 38 And
after these things, Joseph of Arimathea (because he was a disciple
of Jesus, but secretly for fear of the Jews) besought Pilate that he
might take away the body of Jesus. And Pilate gave leave. He came
therefore, and took away the body of Jesus. 39 And Nicodemus also
came, (he who at the first came to Jesus by night,) bringing a mixture of myrrh and aloes, about an hundred pound weight. 40 They
took therefore the body of Jesus, and bound it in linen cloths, with
the spices, as the manner of the Jews is to bury.

41 **Now there was in the place where he was crucified, a
garden; and in the garden a new sepulchre, wherein no man
yet had been laid.** 42 **There, therefore, because of the parasceve
of the Jews, they laid Jesus, because the sepulchre was nigh at
hand.**

Reading with St. Augustine

"The evangelist used a carefully chosen word, with the result that he didn't say that he pierced his side or that he wounded it or anything else but that he opened it, so that in that way the door of life would somehow be thrown open, from which the sacraments of the Church flowed out, without which there is no entryway to the life that is the true life" (*Homilies* 120.2).

"Just as in the womb of the Virgin Mary no one was conceived before him and no one after him, neither was anyone buried in this tomb before him or after him" (*Homilies* 120.5).

MEDITATIO

The sky darkened as the soldiers prepared to break the legs of the crucified men, hastening their deaths before the Sabbath. But when they came to Jesus, they found Him already dead. One soldier, perhaps out of duty or curiosity, thrust his spear into Jesus's side. Blood and water flowed out—a mysterious sign, unnoticed by many but rich with meaning for all time.

St. Augustine sees in this moment the wellspring of the Church's sacraments. The Blood and water from Jesus's pierced side represent Baptism and the Eucharist—sacraments that cleanse and nourish the soul, giving life through His death. The temple of His Body, once foretold, now stands open, its door pierced to flood the world with divine grace.

Nearby, Nicodemus, no longer fearful, approached with Joseph of Arimathea to claim Jesus's Body. The man who once came to Jesus by night now walked in daylight, bearing precious spices for burial. They laid Jesus in a new tomb, unused and pure—mirroring the virgin womb that first bore Him.

Jesus dies in the same way He comes into the world. God had marked this as a miracle. Just as Mary was prepared from her immaculate conception to be the Mother of God, so the tomb was prepared for the Resurrection. The lifeless Flesh laid within would rise, glorified, breaking death's hold forever.

The Cross spoke its final word through the open side of Christ. Blood and water flowed, washing away sin, sealing the promise of eternal life. The pierced Body became the living temple, its door opened wide—not for a chosen few, but for the whole world, called to enter through His sacrifice into life everlasting.

ORATIO

1. Longinus is the traditional name of the Roman soldier who opens Jesus's side. He is simply obeying orders and cannot comprehend the weight of his action. Let me bring to mind occasions in which I do not at first recognize that I was doing God's will in a special way, for myself or someone else, and praise God for all the ways He is using me to help others in ways I will never recognize in this life.

2. Likewise, Joseph of Arimathea and Nicodemus cannot understand how important their actions are in burying Jesus. They are simply performing a corporal work of mercy. I may know of times when, in doing a work of mercy for others, I have helped them. Let me thank God for this and for all the times I may not even have consciously thought I was acting mercifully for others.

3. Augustine compares the open side of Christ to Adam's open side from which Eve came and to the door in Noah's ark through which the animals are saved. Where and in what way has God opened the door of salvation for me?

CONTEMPLATIO

LECTIO: JOHN 20:1–18

Subject: Clinging to Christ in the Spirit

1 And on the first day of the week, Mary Magdalen cometh early,
when it was yet dark, unto the sepulchre; and she saw the stone
taken away from the sepulchre. 2 She ran, therefore, and cometh
to Simon Peter, and to the other disciple whom Jesus loved, and
saith to them: They have taken away the Lord out of the sepulchre,
and we know not where they have laid him. 3 Peter therefore went
out, and that other disciple, and they came to the sepulchre. 4 And
they both ran together, and that other disciple did outrun Peter,
and came first to the sepulchre. 5 And when he stooped down, he
saw the linen cloths lying; but yet he went not in.

6 Then cometh Simon Peter, following him, and went into the
sepulchre, and saw the linen cloths lying, 7 And the napkin that
had been about his head, not lying with the linen cloths, but apart,
wrapped up into one place. 8 Then that other disciple also went in,
who came first to the sepulchre: and he saw, and believed. 9 For as
yet they knew not the scripture, that he must rise again from the
dead. 10 The disciples therefore departed again to their home.

11 But Mary stood at the sepulchre without, weeping. Now
as she was weeping, she stooped down, and looked into the sepulchre, 12 And she saw two angels in white, sitting, one at the head,
and one at the feet, where the body of Jesus had been laid. 13 They
say to her: Woman, why weepest thou? She saith to them: Because
they have taken away my Lord; and I know not where they have
laid him. 14 When she had thus said, she turned herself back, and
saw Jesus standing; and she knew not that it was Jesus. 15 **Jesus
saith to her: Woman, why weepest thou? whom seekest thou?
She, thinking that it was the gardener, saith to him: Sir, if thou
hast taken him hence, tell me where thou hast laid him, and I
will take him away.**

16 **Jesus saith to her: Mary. She turning, saith to him: Rabboni (which is to say, Master).** 17 **Jesus saith to her: Do not
touch me, for I am not yet ascended to my Father. But go to my
brethren, and say to them: I ascend to my Father and to your
Father,** to my God and to your God. 18 Mary Magdalen cometh,
and telleth the disciples: I have seen the Lord, and these things he
said to me.

Reading with St. Augustine

Augustine raises the point that Mary Magdalen calls the One she thinks is a gardener "Sir." This is simply a sign of respect to the man. When she recognizes her true Lord, she calls Him "Teacher" (*Rabboni*), because He has taught her to distinguish human and divine things (see *Homilies* 121.2).

Augustine distinguishes two types of touching: physical touch and mental touch. Jesus lets the disciples, including His female disciples, touch Him in other accounts of the Resurrection. Mary Magdalen is weeping carnally for One she has lost and regained in the Flesh. Jesus wants her not to hold on to Him with carnal affection (see *Homilies* 121.3).

Jesus makes a distinction in the Fatherhood of God, saying "I ascend to my Father and to your Father." Augustine says that God is Father in different ways: to Christ by nature and to us by grace (see *Homilies* 121.3).

MEDITATIO

Three disciples of Jesus—Peter, John, and Mary Magdalen—encounter the risen Christ in different ways. For Peter and John, He is first an absence; the empty tomb is a symbol of their pain taken away. In place of loss is curiosity. The absent Body of Jesus is moving these two men to faith so that when He does appear, they can receive Him with joy.

Mary Magdalen, the main character of this episode, sees Christ not in absence but in disguise. He speaks to her, and she thinks He is a gardener. Mary Magdalen sees with eyes of flesh. She does not even recognize the angels as such; when they speak to her, she responds with worry about Jesus's Body. When Jesus speaks to her, disguised as the gardener, He asks her, "Whom seekest thou?"—the same question Jesus asks the disciples of John the Baptist when Jesus first walks among them (see John 1:38). Jesus teaches Mary Magdalen to see with eyes of faith, not eyes of flesh. Even when she recognizes Him in the Flesh, she should not cling to Him in this way.

Jesus reiterates His point, that the disciples should now see with spiritual eyes and cling to Christ spiritually, when He states the difference in their relationship to the Father. God is their Father by grace, not genetics, and by clinging to the risen Christ in spirit, not with human affection, they can ascend to the Father in spirit.

ORATIO

1. The risen Christ is absent to Peter and John and disguised to Mary Magdalen. In what ways in my life has Jesus led me to Himself through absence and disguise?

2. Mary Magdalen receives a great consolation when she recognizes Christ, and He instructs her to move onward from this. Consolations and desolations come and go in the spiritual life. Are there any consolations or desolations to which I have clung for too long?

3. Physical affection is a passing way to express enduring love among human beings. Do I rely on it too heavily, or on the contrary, do I withhold it from others?

CONTEMPLATIO

LECTIO: JOHN 20:19–31

Subject: Consolation and Desolation

19 **Now when it was late that same day, the first of the week, and the doors were shut, where the disciples were gathered together, for fear of the Jews, Jesus came and stood in the midst, and said to them: Peace be to you.** 20 **And when he had said this, he shewed them his hands and his side.** The disciples therefore were glad, when they saw the Lord.

21 He said therefore to them again: Peace be to you. As the Father hath sent me, I also send you. 22 **When he had said this, he breathed on them; and he said to them: Receive ye the Holy Ghost.** 23 Whose sins you shall forgive, they are forgiven them: and whose sins you shall retain, they are retained. 24 Now Thomas, one of the twelve, who is called Didymus, was not with them when Jesus came. 25 The other disciples therefore said to him: We have seen the Lord. But he said to them: Except I shall see in his hands the print of the nails, and put my finger into the place of the nails, and put my hand into his side, I will not believe.

26 And after eight days again his disciples were within, and Thomas with them. Jesus cometh, the doors being shut, and stood in the midst, and said: Peace be to you. 27 **Then he saith to Thomas: Put in thy finger hither, and see my hands; and bring hither thy hand, and put it into my side; and be not faithless, but believing.** 28 **Thomas answered, and said to him: My Lord, and my God.** 29 **Jesus saith to him: Because thou hast seen me, Thomas, thou hast believed: blessed are they that have not seen, and have believed.** 30 Many other signs also did Jesus in the sight of his disciples, which are not written in this book.

31 But these are written, that you may believe that Jesus is the Christ, the Son of God: and that believing, you may have life in his name.

Reading with St. Augustine

Jesus shows the disciples His hands and side, for which reason Augustine says, "There the vestiges of the wounds were preserved in order to heal the hearts of doubters. But the locked doors were no obstacle to the mass of a body where divinity was. He at whose birth his mother's virginity remained untouched was certainly able to enter when they were unopened" (*Homilies* 121.4).

By breathing the Holy Spirit on the disciples, Jesus shows that the Holy Spirit is the Spirit of both the Father and the Son (*Homilies* 121.4).

Augustine calls sight the universal sense, based on the way we use language: "Listen and see how good that sounds," and "Taste and see how good that tastes," for example. Thomas is to touch and see. Whether he really touches Jesus or not (a debate even in Augustine's time), the point is that believing without the sense of sight is what Jesus commends (*Homilies* 121.5).

MEDITATIO

The disciples huddled together in the locked room, still haunted by fear. The memory of Jesus's crucifixion weighed heavily on their hearts. Suddenly, He stood among them—no knock, no creak of the door—just *"Peace be to you."*

Stunned silence filled the room as He showed them His hands and His side, the wounds still open yet transformed. These marks of suffering, now glorious, spoke louder than words: death was defeated. Joy erupted as they realized the impossible—Jesus was alive!

But Jesus did not let them remain in celebration alone. *"As the Father hath sent Me, I also send you."* With these words, He breathed the Holy Ghost upon them, empowering them to forgive sins. Their mission had begun; the wounds that proved Christ's victory would be echoed in their own lives through trials, courage, and eventual martyrdom.

Thomas was absent that night. For a week, he wrestled with doubt, hearing his brothers' joyful claims. He demanded proof: *"Except I shall see . . . I will not believe."*

The following Sunday, Jesus returned. This time, He came for Thomas. *"Put thy finger hither . . . be not faithless, but believing."* Overwhelmed, Thomas fell to his knees: *"My Lord and my God!"*

Jesus's reply resounded through the ages: *"Blessed are they that have not seen, and have believed."* John recorded these events so that all who read may receive the same call—to see with the eyes of faith, to trust in the victory declared by Christ's living wounds, and to carry that faith boldly into the world.

ORATIO

1. Everything Christ has done is to make the world ready to stand before God and see Him as He is. Every consolation to the disciples becomes a point of strength for proclaiming the Gospel. The same is true of every desolation, such as Thomas's disappointment in not seeing Jesus with the others. How have my consolations and desolations made me a more ready disciple?

2. Christ bears open wounds in His undying Body. In what ways does the promise of resurrection and eternal life give me courage to live with open wounds in my heart?

CONTEMPLATIO

LECTIO: JOHN 21:1–14

Subject: Joy at Jesus's Return

1 After this, Jesus shewed himself again to the disciples at the sea of Tiberias. And he shewed himself after this manner. **2 There were together Simon Peter, and Thomas, who is called Didymus, and Nathanael, who was of Cana of Galilee, and the sons of Zebedee, and two others of his disciples. 3 Simon Peter saith to them: I go a fishing. They say to him: We also come with thee.** And they went forth, and entered into the ship: and that night they caught nothing. 4 But when the morning was come, Jesus stood on the shore: yet the disciples knew not that it was Jesus. 5 Jesus therefore said to them: Children, have you any meat? They answered him: No.

6 He saith to them: Cast the net on the right side of the ship, and you shall find. They cast therefore; and now they were not able to draw it, for the multitude of fishes. 7 That disciple therefore whom Jesus loved, said to Peter: It is the Lord. Simon Peter, when he heard that it was the Lord, girt his coat about him, (for he was naked,) and cast himself into the sea. 8 But the other disciples came in the ship, (for they were not far from the land, but as it were two hundred cubits,) dragging the net with fishes. 9 As soon then as they came to land, they saw hot coals lying, and a fish laid thereon, and bread. 10 Jesus saith to them: Bring hither of the fishes which you have now caught.

11 Simon Peter went up, and drew the net to land, full of great fishes, one hundred and fifty-three. And although there were so many, the net was not broken. 12 Jesus saith to them: Come, and dine. And none of them who were at meat, durst ask him: Who art thou? knowing that it was the Lord. 13 And Jesus cometh and taketh bread, and giveth them, and fish in like manner. 14 This is now the third time that Jesus was manifested to his disciples, after he was risen from the dead.

Reading with St. Augustine

Augustine ponders at length why the disciples, after the resurrection of Jesus, go back to the work they were doing before they met Him. His answer is that the Lord Himself suggests the need to provide for themselves, as Paul does during his ministry (as a tentmaker), so that He can provide them with another miracle that reveals truth. First, Augustine sees in the number of disciples present—seven—that this event speaks to the end of the age. Seven are the days of the week and the ages of mankind (see *Homilies* 122.6).

Then, Augustine ponders the number of fish caught, one hundred fifty-three. There are two numbers at the base of this: ten and seven. Ten is the number of the law (the ten commandments). Seven is the number of the Holy Spirit (His seven gifts and seven virtues, for example). These added together make seventeen. When all the numbers that lead up to seventeen are added together, one through seventeen, they make one hundred fifty-three (see *Homilies* 122.8).

Augustine compares this catch of fish to the one at which Jesus calls His first disciples. In the first, every kind of fish, good and bad, comes into the net and the net tears, representing schism (see Luke 5:1–11). This is the age of the Church. In this catch of fish, the net is full only of good fish. Through this miracle, Jesus speaks to them of the Resurrection of the just (see *Homilies* 122.7).

MEDITATIO

Dawn broke over the Sea of Tiberias as seven weary disciples hauled in empty nets. They had labored all night without reward. As the waves lapped against their boat, a figure appeared on the shore—a steady presence amid the restless waters.

"Children, have you any meat?" the voice called.

"No," they answered, their efforts fruitless once again.

"Cast the net on the right side of the ship, and you shall find."

The net plunged into the deep, and suddenly it strained with life—153 fish, impossibly abundant yet unbroken by the weight. Recognition dawned first on John: *"It is the Lord!"* Peter, ever impetuous, leaped into the water, eager to reach Jesus.

On shore, they found a fire already burning, fish and bread prepared by the Lord Himself. *"Come and dine,"* Jesus invited, welcoming them to His table.

St. Augustine sees this scene as a glimpse of the Church at the end of time. The sea is the turbulent world, where the Church labors tirelessly. The 153 fish signify the fullness of humanity gathered through grace, drawn by faith and love. The unbroken net points to the unity of the Church, despite her vast and varied members.

Jesus, standing firm on the shore, represents the stability of eternity. After the toil of earthly life, Christ calls His faithful to Himself, to share in His eternal feast. Here is the Church's hope:

that beyond the night of labor lies the dawn of unending joy, where Christ Himself will say again, *"Come and dine."*

ORATIO

1. John also composes the book of the Apocalypse, which is full of many joy-filled and triumphant images—as well as many frightening ones. Some Christians choose to dwell on the frightening images and look for their manifestation everywhere. How do I imagine the end of the world as Christ has promised it? Does it resemble this scene at all?

2. The disciples work to support themselves until the Church establishes a structure to support her clergy and missionaries. How do I view work—as an end in itself, as a means to support my family, as missionary territory? How do I support the mission materially?

3. Let me imagine myself among the unnamed disciples in the boat with Peter, John, Thomas, and Nathanael. What is my response to hearing that the Lord has returned?

CONTEMPLATIO

LECTIO: JOHN 21:15–25

Subject: Contemplation and Action

[15] **When therefore they had dined, Jesus saith to Simon Peter: Simon, son of John, lovest thou me more than these? He saith to him: Yea, Lord, thou knowest that I love thee. He saith to him: Feed my lambs.** [16] **He saith to him again: Simon, son of John, lovest thou me? He saith to him: Yea, Lord, thou knowest that I love thee. He saith to him: Feed my lambs.** [17] **He said to him the third time: Simon, son of John, lovest thou me? Peter was grieved, because he had said to him the third time: Lovest thou me? And he said to him: Lord, thou knowest all things: thou knowest that I love thee. He said to him: Feed my sheep.** [18] **Amen, amen I say to thee, when thou wast younger, thou didst gird thyself, and didst walk where thou wouldst. But when thou shalt be old, thou shalt stretch forth thy hands, and another shall gird thee, and lead thee whither thou wouldst not.** [19] **And this he said, signifying by what death he should glorify God.** And when he had said this, he saith to him: Follow me. [20] Peter turning about, saw that disciple whom Jesus loved following, who also leaned on his breast at supper, and said: Lord, who is he that shall betray thee?

[21] Him therefore when Peter had seen, he saith to Jesus: Lord, and what shall this man do? [22] **Jesus saith to him: So I will have him to remain till I come, what is it to thee? follow thou me.** [23] This saying therefore went abroad among the brethren, that that disciple should not die. And Jesus did not say to him: He should not die; but, So I will have him to remain till I come, what is it to thee? [24] This is that disciple who giveth testimony of these things, and hath written these things; and we know that his testimony is true. [25] But there are also many other things which Jesus did; which, if they were written every one, the world itself, I think, would not be able to contain the books that should be written.

Reading with St. Augustine

On Peter's confession and Jesus's prediction of Peter's martyrdom: "That denier and lover, elated by his presumption, cast down by his denial, cleansed by weeping, proven by his confession, crowned by suffering, found this end. He found this end so that he would die out of perfect love for the name of him to whom he had promised with impetuous haste that he was going to die. Strengthened by [Christ's] resurrection, let him do what he had promised in his immature weakness. For it was right that Christ would first die for Peter's salvation and that then Peter [would die] for proclaiming Christ" (*Homilies* 123.4).

For Augustine, Peter and John represent the two lives of a Christian: the life of loving, active service to the Lord and the Church in this world (Peter), and the life of being fully loved in contemplation of the Lord in the world to come (John). That John remains until that world comes means that contemplation, though available in part now, is fulfilled only at the end. The Church must live the life of Peter until then: "Let Peter love him, then, so that we may be delivered from this mortality; let John be loved by him, so that we may be saved in that immortality" (*Homilies* 124.5–6).

MEDITATIO

John's gospel concludes where it begins, with an invitation to contemplation. The Word made Flesh walks with two of His disciples, Peter and John, whom He called at the beginning. He walked along the shore with Peter and John, His voice steady over the sound of the waves. After their meal, He turned to Peter with a question that pierced deeper than any wound: *"Simon, son of John, lovest thou Me more than these?"*

"Yea, Lord, thou knowest that I love Thee."

Three times Jesus asked, and three times Peter answered—undoing the sting of his threefold denial. But love is more than words. Jesus gave Peter a mission: *"Feed My lambs . . . Feed My sheep."* In that charge, Peter's life of active service began—not to prove his love, but to live it, strengthened by Christ's forgiveness.

St. Augustine sees Peter as the embodiment of the active Christian life—leading, teaching, suffering, and ultimately dying for Christ. His path is one of sacrifice and action, formed and sustained by the love Christ first showed him.

But John's path is different. He follows silently, listening, seeing. *"What shall this man do?"* Peter asks. Jesus answers, *"If I will have him remain till I come, what is that to thee? Follow thou Me."*

John represents the contemplative life, rooted in spiritual longing and watchful prayer. He waits, listens, and records, bearing witness through the written Word that feeds generations. His long years, marked by exile and revelation, reflect the Church's enduring call to contemplation.

Both lives, Augustine reminds us, flow from the same source—Christ's love. In Peter, we see the Church's mission; in

John, its eternal hope, the buoy of contemplative prayer. Together, fidelity in action and contemplation reveal the fullness of discipleship—a life lived for Christ in service and in longing, until He comes again.

ORATIO

1. Peter fails when he tries to do for Christ what Christ must first do for him. In all that I do as a Christian—in my family, at work, in my church—where has Christ done this first for me? How can I imitate Him there?

2. I have taken the time to meditate with Augustine on John's gospel. Such meditation makes room for contemplation. What has been the fruit of this meditation? Where do I feel God calling me next—to more loving, active service with Peter, to contemplation with John, or some measure of both? What does my life look like concretely so I can respond to God's invitation to love?

CONTEMPLATIO